Credit: Jack Goldsmith

Penguin Canada

**ROOM FOR THOUGHT**

AVI FRIEDMAN is the author of four books, all on housing: *The Grow Home*, *Planning the New Suburbia*, *The Adaptable House*, and *Peeking through the Keyhole* (with David Krawitz). He has written numerous articles on subjects ranging from construction technology to neighbourhood planning for academic and trade publications in both Canada and the United States. His syndicated column has appeared in the CanWest chain of newspapers since August 2000. Friedman's designs for housing prototypes—such as the Grow Home and the Next Home—are renowned internationally for their innovation. He is also the winner of numerous design awards. Friedman lives in Montreal and teaches at the McGill School of Architecture.

## ALSO BY AVI FRIEDMAN

*The Grow Home*

*Planning the New Suburbia*

*The Adaptable House*

*Peeking through the Keyhole* (with David Krawitz)

# ROOM FOR THOUGHT

rethinking home and community design

AVI FRIEDMAN

PENGUIN
CANADA

PENGUIN CANADA

Published by the Penguin Group

Penguin Group (Canada), 90 Eglinton Avenue East, Suite 700, Toronto, Ontario, Canada M4P 2Y3 (a division of Pearson Penguin Canada Inc.)

Penguin Group (USA) Inc., 375 Hudson Street, New York, New York 10014, U.S.A.
Penguin Books Ltd, 80 Strand, London WC2R 0RL, England
Penguin Ireland, 25 St Stephen's Green, Dublin 2, Ireland (a division of Penguin Books Ltd)
Penguin Group (Australia), 250 Camberwell Road, Camberwell, Victoria 3124, Australia (a division of Pearson Australia Group Pty Ltd)
Penguin Books India Pvt Ltd, 11 Community Centre, Panchsheel Park, New Delhi – 110 017, India
Penguin Group (NZ), cnr Airborne and Rosedale Roads, Albany, Auckland 1310, New Zealand (a division of Pearson New Zealand Ltd)
Penguin Books (South Africa) (Pty) Ltd, 24 Sturdee Avenue, Rosebank, Johannesburg 2196, South Africa

Penguin Books Ltd, Registered Offices: 80 Strand, London WC2R 0RL, England

First published 2005

(WEB) 10 9 8 7 6 5 4 3 2 1

Manufactured in Canada.

LIBRARY AND ARCHIVES CANADA CATALOGUING IN PUBLICATION

Friedman, Avi, 1952–
    Room for thought / Avi Friedman.

ISBN 0-14-305004-4

1. City planning—Social aspects. 2. Architecture, Domestic—Social aspects. I. Title.

HT166.F737 2005      307.1'216      C2005-903160-3

Visit the Penguin Group (Canada) website at **www.penguin.ca**

*In memory of my father*
*Haim Friedman*

# CONTENTS

ix    Places of Departure

## LOOKING HOMEWARD

2     A Home Fit for a Queen

12    Dormers in Dalian

22    To Keep or Not to Keep the Living and Dining Rooms?

32    A Conversation with Your Fridge

42    Oversized Furniture or Small Rooms?

50    Timeless Design

60    Homes with a Global Reach

## THERE GOES THE NEIGHBORHOOD

72    Living Above the Store

82    Designing for Civility

92    Bring Back the Scale

104   Reinventing Cities

114   Housing the Trees

## NUTS AND JOISTS

126   They Don't Build Them Like They Used To

138   Weathering the Storm

148   A Home in a Box

158   A Margarine Container Deck

**IN PERSON**

170  Accepting the Orange Tile

182  Beaulieu's Race

194  Our First Home

206  Design for Family Life

214  Housing the Rest of My Life


225  Acknowledgments

227  Bibliography

235  Illustration Credits

# PLACES OF DEPARTURE

The Israeli town of Petach Tikva, where I was born, has a plow and an orange tree as its emblem. Orange groves and plowed fields are my childhood memories. For ten years I lived in a neighborhood on the edge of Petach Tikva. My first recollections of a home, groups of homes, the space in between, and the space around were all established in that town. There, I experienced firsts of everything. Many of the images my mind registered have stayed and traveled with me throughout my career as an architect. They later helped me form my own perceptions of home and community.

I hardly remember my first home, a room tacked onto the back of an existing single-story dwelling. My parents, who had just arrived in the newly established state from Europe, were fortunate to find a place to live, unlike so many immigrants who were initially housed in barracks and tents. The neighborhood, to which we moved when I was three, was built to house immigrants like my parents.

Our home was a unit in a cinderblock four-family walk-up. The 350-square-foot (33-square-meter) apartment had a hallway, a small kitchen off the entrance, a living room that doubled as my parents' sleeping quarters, and another, smaller bedroom. Wintry nights were spent in the tiny kitchen with a corner kerosene heater, listening to my parents' stories from the old country until it was time to go to bed. I slept on a pull-down bed in the room I shared with my sister.

What I recall most about my childhood place was the outdoors: the space behind the buildings, the narrow streets, the backyards, the small public parks, and the orange groves that surrounded us. It was the simplicity of this urban landscape that made it unique. The homes were laid out parallel to each other with shared public green yards in between. Our home bordered the daycare I attended and a playground where I played with my friends after school.

A four-shop strip mall with a red-tiled roof was located in the heart of the neighborhood. I walked there every day, a cotton bag and shopping list in hand. The tiny grocery store was packed to the ceiling, and the easy familiarity and daily conversations among its patrons made it as much a community center as a store. Along with the three other establishments—a butcher, a barber, and a variety store—it seemed to satisfy the basic necessities of our small neighborhood.

A clinic was built a short distance away. This was the place where I got my inoculation shots and had my yearly medical checkups. An elementary school was constructed in the vicinity not long after. I used to walk there, and cherished strolling back home with my friends in the early afternoons. There was a sense of togetherness in our community. People knew and cared about each other. Few owned a car back then, and the bus stop was where people would talk about each other and everything else as they waited for the bus to take them to town.

When I was ten we moved to Tel Aviv, Israel's largest city. Stretching along the Mediterranean, it was, and still is, a bustling place. The busy streets overflowing with urban life were a shock to the system after the placid Petach Tikva. We lived in a fourth-floor apartment above a department store, in one of the city's liveliest commercial streets. I had difficulty adjusting to my new surroundings. I missed the orange orchard, the open fields, and the green spaces between the fourplexes. With time, though, I came to appreciate the many advantages that a city had to offer: the public parks, the cultural hubs, the markets, the alleyways. Summers were spent at the beach, to which I walked from home daily with my friends. The open blue sea was the place where dreams were modeled with sand and imaginary building ideas born.

My first notions of home, community, and city life were formed in Petach Tikva and in Tel Aviv. The memory of these places accompanied me as I continued my life's journey, and later when I began my formal training as an architect. Over the years, these memories served as a sound departure point to many of my own designs for homes and communities.

What galvanized my views as an architect and as a planner was the firm belief that homes and neighborhoods are first and foremost about people, and that we view our surroundings differently as our own lives change. Growing up in a small home and a close-knit community inspired my social sense as well as my sense of space. Stories that I heard from my parents on chilly evenings in our cramped kitchen were etched in my memory along with the moments themselves.

My childhood surroundings also taught me a valuable lesson about human scale. Walking in narrow streets, markets, and squares made me realize that a building is merely one aspect of what makes a place comfortable. It's how each building relates to the next and the space in between that creates a comfortable place. When a home is designed, or a community planned, the lives that will unfold in them are as important as the architectural concept they attempt to express. Proportions, materials, and light will all be backstage to the interactions between people.

It is these types of observations, relationships, and moments that I have recalled in the essays gathered here. They are about the points where design touches life, and about the big and small things that make us appreciate, or become discontented with, our homes and neighborhoods.

My formal architectural training took me to the city of Milan, the Israeli town of Haifa on the slopes of Mount Carmel, and the cosmopolitan island city of Montreal. When I looked for a home in those cities, I always searched for places whose urban features were similar to those of my childhood landscapes. In Montreal, where I finally settled, started my own family, and worked, I have lived in a neighborhood where the streets are narrow, the homes are close to each other, people walk to corner stores, and neighbors greet one another.

The places I have called home are different from the houses built on the suburban edge of town. When I first saw these developments, I questioned their design and the values they represent. Being born and having lived elsewhere, I wondered how and why we've drifted away from reason and what these suburban settings and architectural forms have to do with current societal concerns. In my own design work and writing I try to offer an alternative to current practices and to sensitize people to the consequences of our chosen way of living.

The topics in this book question the foundations of home design and neighborhood planning. I have attempted to trace their historical roots but, more so, to cast a new light for their better appreciation. The essays have been assembled in four parts. The first touches on domestic issues and centers on the home. Next, the neighborhood and the city are visited and explored. The mechanics of the home are discussed in the next section, and my personal endeavors as an architect, homeowner, and parent conclude this collection.

# LOOKING HOMEWARD

# A HOME FIT FOR A QUEEN

AS I STROLLED ALONG THE VISITOR'S PATH AND ADMIRED THE palatial rooms of Windsor Castle, I recalled some of the rooms in the homes I've lived in over the years. I'd been invited to Windsor to participate in a conference that focused on giving citizens a better say in the governance of their communities. Along with other experts I engaged in discussions and debated global issues in this magnificent setting. For three days I lived in a small room in the St. George's guest house on the castle grounds and repeatedly returned to view the Queen's residence.

As I gazed at a display of shining swords and armor in the castle's imposing hallway, I remembered the tiny hall in our first home where the table on which my sister and I did our homework stood. The Queen's tennis-court-sized dining room with its elaborate wall and ceiling woodwork brought back memories of the apartment we moved to in later years, where my father sawed the edges of a narrow table to make it fit the kitchen's cramped dining space. Before each meal we had to pull the table away from the wall to make room for my sister to squeeze in.

The intricate gold-painted plasterwork on the bedroom's ceiling and its artwork drew sounds of admiration from the visitors in

Windsor. The tall, hand-carved wooden bed took me back to our small living room in Petach Tikva which doubled as my parents' bedroom each night. My father would pull out the sitting portion of the sofa and turn over the back to make a double bed. In the King's vast reception hall where he attended to commoners' requests while sitting on a carved ivory throne—a gift of an Indian prince—I thought of the room I rented from Signora Pozzi in Milan, where I studied architecture. In the middle of the room where I slept and washed was a round table on which I ate, drew, and wrote my papers.

I've lived in larger homes since and designed a few myself, but still, I've never quite understood the obsession with large homes. I was puzzled by North Americans' desire to house themselves so spaciously. Their wish to live in a scaled-down version of Windsor Castle intrigued me. I wondered if it was an expression of wealth or a craving for higher social status that makes people buy these monster homes. And does easy access to financial credit have something to do with it? Is their house size really the homebuyers' choice, or are they obliged to buy these dwellings because smaller houses aren't available? The average size of North American households has shrunk in recent years, so why do families still upgrade and buy even larger homes?

Home-buying decisions are complex and influenced by a number of factors, of course, but perhaps the search for large homes is rooted in the places from which people immigrated to North America and their aspirations for a better life.

Many of the first settlers of this continent came from highly populated urban settings. The poverty-stricken newcomers who crossed oceans hadn't owned land or homes in their native countries. North America wasn't only the land of opportunity, but a vast place where land was plentiful and cheap. At first, new arrivals lived in crowded cities along the Atlantic coast. But many dared to migrate into the hinterland and settle it, developing what later became known as the frontier mentality. Along with land ownership came homeownership. Houses built in rural areas had no size restrictions or zoning limits; their size was mostly governed by how much the owner could afford to spend. This mindset has not subsided. Immigrants are still drawn to this continent by the opportunities the place offers, chief among them homeownership. A home of one's own is, after all, the core of the American Dream.

But perhaps the most compelling explanation of swelling house size lies in the evolution of homeownership since then. Before the devastation of the Great Depression, governments believed that housing was essentially the responsibility of the free market. Pressure for housing assistance and economic recovery during the crisis of the 1930s compelled governments to reconsider this position. The United States took an aggressive stance toward housing when, in 1933, it established the Home Owners' Loan Corporation to provide refinancing for households that faced foreclosure and to recover properties that had already been defaulted on. A year later another New Deal program, the National Housing Act, created the Federal Housing Administration. The FHA eased the pressure of the immense housing demand by insuring long-term fully amortized mortgages provided by private lenders. Reducing lenders' risk in this way boosted their willingness to lend while limiting down-payment requirements and interest rates.

Homeownership, in other words, was opened up to the working class, and soon the suburban family with a new house and a long-term FHA debt became the symbol of the American way. Largely through FHA programs, equity was introduced to the estates of thirty-five million households between 1933 and 1978. The flip side of this institutionalized suburbanization, though, was the loss from urban centers of middle-class citizens—and middle-class stability.

The FHA's conservative policies strongly favored single-family over multi-family dwellings and new construction over rehabilitation of existing units. Rampant consumerism following the Second World War, coupled with the great number of returning GIs and the baby boom that followed closely thereafter, created a terrific housing demand. This demand was reinforced by the United States government's official support of the view that sixteen million GIs should return to civilian life with a home of their own. As part of the 1944 GI Bill of Rights the Veteran's Administration created a mortgage guarantee program, further bolstering the demand for owner-occupied units by enabling veterans to borrow the entire appraised value of a house. The most conservative of FHA estimates indicated that responding to this demand would immediately require the construction of five million new units, with a total of 12.5 million over the following decade. Traditional approaches to housing development—numerous small-scale builders with their teams of specialized laborers—would be insufficient for the task. The need for change was clear.

Governments responded with assurances and financing programs that would make it profitable for private developers to build mass-produced subdivisions on vast tracts of land. The banking industry, as a result, began to play a critical role in home building. Since the amount of money that people were willing and able to pay month after month was integral to the type of house they'd buy, a multitude of design strategies were all aimed at obtaining that magic number. Surprisingly, some of these strategies—such as smaller homes on small lots and with unfinished parts—went against the grain of conventional financial wisdom. Bankers preferred home-buyers who could commit themselves to a large loan, as long as it was paid back. Potential buyers were, in fact, encouraged to borrow. When the modern mortgage system was set up in the years following the Second World War, regulators allowed 25 percent of a combined household income to be allocated for shelter expenses (mortgage payments, municipal taxes, and heating). It was assumed that the remaining 75 percent would be spent on other basic household expenses such as food, education, and old-age savings. The 1950s saw a large number of first-time homebuyers lining up outside model homes across North America. As the husband was usually the only breadwinner in the family, the 25 percent for shelter would come from his income.

Fast-forward a decade or two. The 1970s saw the return of many women to the labor force, and most families now had two pay checks. Financial regulators recognized this trend, and upped the allowable shelter allocation to 32 percent of the now-enlarged total household income. In real terms, homebuyers were allowed to spend much more on housing.

Builders didn't miss a beat. They knew that a higher disposable income meant being able to spend more on a home. There's no comparison, then, between the homes they've built since the 1970s and those that were constructed at the beginning of the mass-consumption housing market of the 1950s. Back then, middle-class homeownership was considered one of the greatest postwar achievements. Tract homes with few amenities were meant to satisfy the basic needs of a young family. Such a modest beginning, it was argued, would be a stepping stone toward the acquisition of larger, better-equipped homes. In 1943 an average home measured 800 square feet (80 square meters); in 1955 it had reached 1,100 square feet (110 square meters). By the mid-1980s, when the baby boomers began to buy their homes, single-family house sizes were close to 2,000 square feet (200 square meters). This expansion came hand in hand with a decrease in the size of the average Canadian household, from 3.9 members in 1961 to 2.6 in 2001. Simply put, since the postwar era we've gradually increased the amount of space per person. We've reduced what experts call our *measure of crowding.*

Builders didn't stop at larger houses; they loaded them up with costly features and gadgets. Contemporary home design reflects this trend. If the postwar house provided a shelter, today's home is a gateway to social status. New developments in comparable demographic areas vie with one another to appear different; paradoxically, their basic interiors and attention-grabbing features are all the same. Detailed craftsmanship has been replaced with a huge foyer, high ceilings, tall windows, curving staircases, and fireplaces destined to be used only rarely. Modern homes in new developments are presented as a parade of wonders. Every room is designed to simplify life and astound a visitor.

Consider, for instance, the kitchen. Builders and real estate agents regard them as "sellers" of new and old homes alike. The kitchen must be big, they all attest. New fridge models with double doors have been introduced. Along with the dishwasher, the microwave has moved in to occupy space among the cabinets, joining an even larger-sized oven. The dining portion of the kitchen has been transformed from a modest nook to a full-fledged breakfast area with a larger table and a bar-with-stools arrangement. Ironically, as kitchens have expanded so too have eating out and ordering food in.

Clever marketing and consumer demand have transformed other rooms as well. The once-humble bathroom now boasts a veritable spa of appliances: a whirlpool bath, multi-jet shower, silent-flush toilet, and double-sink counter with a row of theater makeup lights demand our attention in an Italian-tiled paradise. And the main bathroom is just one of many; a couple of powder rooms, one on each level, and an en-suite bathroom off the master bedroom complete the picture.

With too much space on their hands and too few uses, builders have even invented new functions. "Media rooms" are designated to house our electronics. The leftover space next to the kitchen has become the "great room" (not to be confused with the family room), and the "bonus room" came to life when builders ran out of names.

The media have played a pivotal role in expanding our interest in home design and decor. From a modest beginning in magazines like *Better Homes and Gardens,* the rise of the home as fashion cachet has been staggering. Such publications as *Martha Stewart Living, Canadian Living,* and *Architectural Digest* attempt not only to inform homeowners about decoration but to encourage them toward a tailored lifestyle. Targeted broadcasting appeals to renovation buffs, decor enthusiasts, and buyers of dream homes on beach resorts. Reality TV has introduced viewers to the living rooms, bedrooms, and bathrooms of both wealthy and ordinary North Americans. Homes have become entertainment, crossing another threshold in promoting consumption of space and content.

Municipal zoning bylaws haven't made things any easier for buyers who search for smaller homes and the builders who are willing to build them. Houses have become the main source of the suburbs' municipal revenue. Taxation is based on property evaluation, of which size is the determining factor. Owners of small homes, then, pay less than owners of large ones, yet use the same municipal services. Unsurprisingly, developments with typical lots measuring a whopping 60 by 100 feet (18 by 30 meters) have become the norm in suburbia. When a request is placed before city council for a permit to build higher-density developments made up of smaller, lower-cost homes, the prevailing sentiment is NIMBY (not in my backyard).

The demand for large homes has not, and likely will not, subside; people will continue to spend more time at home and more money on comfort. Designers, appliance manufacturers, and builders will be hard at work searching for modes and means to draw homebuyers to model homes, where they'll be less likely to ask themselves if they really need it.

The years ahead, however, will be marked by the retirement of the baby boom generation. And with their offspring buying their own homes, will the boomers still need those large houses? And then there's homebuyer diversity: a sizable number of people searching for homes today are singles, couples without children, and single-parent families. Will *they* need such an abundance of space?

Driving through new housing developments on my way back from the airport—images of that castle's grandeur still fresh in my mind—made me think that perhaps every North American does want a home fit for a queen.

# DORMERS IN DALIAN

STILL JETLAGGED, I WAS DRIVEN FROM THE FURAMA HOTEL IN Dalian, China, where I had arrived a few hours earlier to partici- pate in a United Nations–sponsored housing conference. My guide insisted that I visit a certain housing project in this city of six million people. As the car made its way to the outskirts of town, I watched the bustling streets curiously. Dalian was one of China's new development zones and was in an accelerated process of modernization. Construction cranes loomed over the city and Renmin Road, the main boulevard. The towering office buildings, aluminum and reflective glass exteriors shining in the sun, looked as if their designers had recycled blueprints of New York, Tokyo, or Toronto buildings. People bustled in and out of their granite- covered lobbies, nodding to porters who held the door open.

Soon after we left the downtown the landscape began to open up. The roadside trees and shrubs were meticulously kept, and every once in a while we'd pass a street sweeper wearing a white surgi- cal mask. As we drove along a coastal road my guide, a young English literature student, pointed out landmarks and described their importance. The driver began to slow down and brought the car to a stop at the roadside. We stepped out and walked a bit. Ahead of us was a cluster of North American–style homes. The cottages were clad with brown clay bricks and had sloped roofs with two dormers equally spaced in the roof's center. What were these Western suburban homes doing in Dalian? I wondered. My guide, noticing my amazement, said quietly, "Even in design we're catching up with you."

As I circled one of the houses I reflected on what gap she was referring to. Did she mean the East–West cultural divide? Was there a style gap that had to be bridged at all? On this, my first trip to China, had I really expected to see pagoda-like houses with pointy edges? And then there was the issue of architectural heritage: I wondered if Chinese architects weren't concerned about the prospect of losing their country's architectural identity and long building tradition. In this age of global trade, is global culture inevitable?

A cross-border architectural style was first proposed by architects almost a century ago. It began with the Bauhaus, a German school of design and architecture founded in 1919 and headed by Walter Gropius. Bauhaus architects favored practical design choices that also kept the cost down. Rejecting cornices, eaves, and other decorative details, they employed principles of classical architecture in its simplest and purest form. Flat roofs, square building shapes, and plain furniture over more ostentatious and ornamental components were some of the Bauhaus style trademarks. With the rise of Nazism in the 1930s, though, the school shut down and its founders moved to America.

The movement transformed and was renamed International Style after the 1932 book *The International Style,* written by historian Henry-Russell Hitchcock and architect Philip Johnson and published to accompany a Museum of Modern Art exhibition. A typical example of International Style is New York's thirty-eight-story Seagram Building, designed by Mies Van der Rohe and completed in 1958. Set on metal-clad columns, the facade consists of bronze plates and tinted glass. The building has floor-to-ceiling windows, making the exterior wall into a curtain, as envisioned by the Bauhaus architects.

China, I surmised, was at a stage that the European and North American continents were at a century ago: in the midst of transition between architectural styles. Just as the West had attempted to shed traces of its dominating Victorian architecture, today Dalian homes embody China's need to close style ranks with the rest of the world. And China was facing another milestone, one that North America had undergone in the middle of the twentieth century: the transformation of homes into consumption goods. Whereas a century ago several generations would live in the same family home, today people move about more frequently, following job opportunities and the upward social mobility they represent.

North American housing developers have responded in kind. Over the past half-century they have gradually replaced the form, materials, and layouts that originated in local tradition or the designer's birthplace with more homogeneous and commonly recognizable features. Vernacular and local styles have slowly started to erode and fade, the only exception being regional design variations resulting from climatic differences. The design of homes in tract projects, it seems, has to be familiar to new and subsequent buyers.

Changes in production and distribution of building products have also contributed to homogeneity. Doors, windows, exterior cladding, and roofing products are now manufactured by multi-national corporations that market identical items nationally and even internationally. The Warroad, Minnesota–based company Marvin Windows and Doors Inc., for example, exports its products to over fifty countries around the world. American Standard also exports its plumbing fixtures to numerous countries in several continents. Even at the product level, then, regionalism is rapidly diminishing.

The media play an important role in this cross-border dissemination of design styles. Feature articles on best-selling homes in national magazines help spread ideas from coast to coast. Popular magazines on home style and decor are found in newsstands around the world, and some are translated into several languages. Cable channels broadcast new home-building and renovation programs nationally and internationally. Based mostly in North America, these media outlets have contributed to the proliferation of Western building styles.

Architectural firms and building development corporations also cross borders. North American firms are designing projects in

Asian cities whose civic leaders strive to lend these places a Western look. Some mayors even promote the fact that a local project has been designed by an internationally renowned architect. The Guggenheim Museum in Bilbao, by Los Angeles–based architect Frank O. Gehry, has been so successful in attracting visitors from afar to the Spanish city that it's opened a watershed of opportunities for cross-border architecture. In residential design, the single detached house with a multi-gable roof and a two-car garage up front—a cross between Victorian and modern styles—can be found in widely differing locales, China among them. Inside the home itself, even the powder room, originally introduced in a northern climate and meant to be used upon entry, is featured in residences located in Asian cities with mild weather.

In North America's suburban landscape, exterior design differences, if they exist, are minor and frequently economically driven. Styles are often altered in order to make a house look more spacious than it really is. Architects of custom-designed houses offer a choice of different facades—from modest to ostentatious—to reflect the homeowner's personality. The exteriors even of tract housing developments have offered some variety in recent years. But for the most part homebuyers are given, at best, the choice of a shade of brick or of garage door color; they tend to have very little say in the matter and are at the mercy of the developer.

Along with the swelling size of homes has come the mushrooming of the facade area. Compared with homes of earlier decades,

newly built homes—with at least 40 percent of their front elevation allocated to the garage door—have lost their grace. Little
area is left for anything else. Placing an entrance door in the
middle of a home or installing a picture window in the living
room to let in more light is hard to do once a two- or three-car
garage occupies a sizable chunk of the front wall.

And then there's the ongoing search for a winning style. Over
the years a blend of modern and Victorian styles has domi-
nated the suburban landscape, with little attempt made to expand
this hybrid vocabulary and explore other styles. Although no one
has ever conducted a thorough survey of what style homebuyers
really like, builders often claim that the hybrid style is what
people most prefer. The resulting endless repetition has made
most streetscapes dull—at times even grotesque.

One can only wonder whether in the not-so-distant future
we'll have any taste of the local flavor left, if we've forever lost
the craftsmanship and style that once distinguished one place
from another. Architectural vocabulary is no different from
endangered natural species or uncommon languages. New buildings in existing communities can respect the character of the
old. Contemporary designs need not emulate them, nor create a
Disneyworld environment, but simply respect their scale, volume,
and materials. In a global age, unique architectural style is what
lends to a place and its residents a sense of self.

I had an opportunity to develop urban and architectural
guidelines to ensure that the new would fit in with the old.

The invitation came from the village council of the tiny Quebec town of Senneville, on the western tip of the Island of Montreal. They were concerned about the building of several trophy mansions by recent well-to-do arrivals. Monster homes all, they lacked the grace that characterizes the old architecture of Senneville.

A drive along Senneville Road, the main thoroughfare, is like a tour through the architectural history of Canada. The village was established as a trading post in 1672, and developed as a place for summer homes of wealthy Montrealers in the middle of the nineteenth century. Today Senneville is a pleasant mix of vast country mansions, modest rural dwellings, and post–Second World War houses that cleverly borrow from the other two types. A number of architectural styles are visible throughout the village. The vernacular style, marked by large outdoor galleries under sloping roofs supported by columns, can be found both in rustic homes built a century ago and in houses built in the last few decades. Homes in the rural style have stone walls with square openings and steep gable roofs with dormers. The only difference between these houses and the postwar versions is the size of the lots: the older houses are sited on ample pieces of land while the newer lots are more in keeping with postwar suburban dimensions. Many of the characteristics of the Arts and Crafts movement, incorporated so skillfully by the architects Edward and William Maxwell in their designs for the grand properties of Senneville built at the turn of the last century, are echoed in more recent homes as well.

How then did I decide to prepare Senneville for the future? By learning from the past. The old homes were designed by architects who offered innovation within traditional guidelines, and this would form the basis of my own approach. I led a team of researchers that visited each of the 350 homes in the community. We studied building proportions, articulation of brick and stone on the facades, types of windows and doors, roof shapes and angles, dormers and other roof elements, ancillary structures and their relation to the main house, and finally the local landscape, including trees and shrubs. This architectural detective work led to a wealth of information, most of which turned out to be hidden treasure.

The small community of Senneville had, we discovered, fully six character zones, each with its own unique historic features. Future additions to existing homes, new homes, and even large developments would have to respect these traits. Detailed design guidelines were prepared for each zone, specifying the essential components that future architects would have to bear in mind and follow.

Will these guidelines limit creativity and lead to a theme-park-like environment in Senneville? No, I don't think so. The village will no doubt have to make firm decisions to articulate its future character. Should the floodgates be opened up to let an anything-goes style prevail, or should certain restrictions apply? Good guidelines, I trust, will allow for a framework of diversity within harmony. Be it in Dalian or in Senneville, architects and developers, as well as future residents, need to appreciate that the future is often built upon the foundation of the past. The architectural and urban character is no exception.

# TO KEEP OR NOT TO KEEP THE LIVING AND DINING ROOMS?

SPECULATIVE BUILDERS REFER TO HOMES AS *PRODUCTS*. WHEREAS homebuyers see their lives unfolding in residences, builders have a nearer horizon. They have to sell and build quickly and move on to the next project; handing over the keys is their ultimate goal. A model home—the showcase of a new development, like a new model in a car dealership—must therefore look good. It ought to draw a "wow," make an unsure buyer fall in love at first sight, edge out the competition across the street. A hotel-sized kitchen, beautifully lit with stainless steel appliances, will be an anchor; a spacious marble-tiled bathroom with trendy fixtures and a Jacuzzi will be an attention grabber. It's all a question of first impressions.

Despite my experience working with builders, I'm often uneasy when I have to present my design to one. I know their critique will be harsh and thorough. The success or failure of their investment, I feel, rests on the shoulders of my design. Throughout our discussion, the ultimate user of the design, the homeowner, is faceless and is referred to as a *client*.

I parked my car near a newly constructed house in a barren development and stepped into a very cold January afternoon. It was a

Friday, and I could tell that the builder's office receptionist was eager to end the week. The months of January and February are traditionally the busy season in the home-building business, since people tend to buy houses for summer occupancy. The number of sales during these months determines the year's overall activity. So designs are rushed, finalized, and made ready for buyers to see and purchase.

From inside the builder's private office I could hear one end of a heated telephone conversation. I headed to an empty seat in the anteroom and waited. It sounded as if Jack, the builder, was in the midst of an argument with his banker about interest he was being charged on a line of credit. He wasn't likely to be in a good mood when he saw me.

The call finally ended. Jack stepped out to instruct his secretary, noticed me, and asked me to come in. He was an experienced builder who built primarily for the move-up market—those who had sold their first small house and were buying a bigger one. He referred to his homes as Oldsmobiles: large, comfortable, yet not too expensive. This time, though, he was about to start a housing development made up of entry-level homes that would appeal to young couples with a modest income. I'd been recognized for my design of affordable housing, expertise that Jack wanted me to apply to this project.

After a brief greeting, Jack cleared his wide desk as he pointed to my roll of drawings and said "Let's see what you have for me today." I unrolled the plans, placed a heavy item on each end, and began to describe the layout of the two-story-plus-basement townhouse. I animated my description by walking him through the unbuilt home as if he were a visitor. He listened to my explanation, cutting me off at times when he thought I'd taken too long. It felt as if his mind was still in conversation with his banker.

"What's the unit's overall area?" he asked. I told him. He pulled a PalmPilot from his pocket and punched in some numbers. "Too expensive," he said. "I'll have trouble selling such a product in this site." That took the wind out of my sails—I'd been hoping to get his approval so that I could prepare the construction documents. Now I might have to begin my design all over again.

"What can we take out to make the home smaller?" he asked. There was silence. Sitting there, mulling over the plans, we pondered which functions we could do without. "I can shrink the kitchen and the main bathroom a bit," I proposed. "You must be kidding. Kitchens and bathrooms are my real estate agents," he said. "I can reduce the parents' bedroom area," I offered. "The parents are paying for this home. Don't start with them," Jack responded quickly. "Maybe you can shrink the living room and knock off the dining room," he suggested after a moment of silence. "In our home," he continued, "hardly anyone ever sits in the living room, and the dining room is never used." "What about holidays and family gatherings?" I asked. "What's the point of keeping valuable space for events that take place only once or twice a year?" Jack said, dismissing my argument. He glanced at his watch and suggested that I reconsider my design and that we meet the following week.

On the drive back to my office I reflected on Jack's comments about the living and dining rooms and his suggestion to do without them. Are these rooms really needed? New lifestyle trends have shifted traditional family schedules, and for many people today it's hard to find time for a formal meal in the dining room on a week night. Setting up the table, carrying the food there, taking time to discuss the day's events, cleaning up, and moving to the living room for coffee and dessert while listening to music—that all seems like an evening from a long-gone era. The use of space at home has also become gradually more decentralized. Do we really need, then, to retain a separate room for an occasion that may occur only once or twice a year? Shouldn't the new trends dictate a new priority list in how homes are used?

In his book *History of Domestic Space,* Peter Ward points out that the living room, which was also called a parlor, salon, sitting room, or front room, was once the place where the family met acquaintances and presented itself to the outside world. It was the home's most public space. When North Americans made their transition from the colonist's one-room house to a home with several rooms, the parlor was added. It could be found even in relatively small homes at the turn of the century. Unlike European homes in the Victorian era, whose parlor was clearly a formal space, on this continent, and mostly in modest residences, the living room had a touch of informality.

This was also the room in which a family would display their material accomplishments and treasured mementos. Paintings, family heirlooms, silverware, and photos were hung on walls and put in glass cases. A piano, according to Peter Ward, was also common in middle-class homes in both Europe and North America. It was a mark of culture and a signal of wealth. Women's musical and vocal talents were highly valued, and playing for guests was part of formal hospitality.

Another key feature in the living room was the fireplace, or hearth, which had several roles. Since it was ornate and expensive to construct, it represented wealth. It also provided warmth and served as a visual focal point, just as the television would in later years. Extended family members or visitors would gather after dinner to chat, play cards, and listen to music played on the piano.

The dining room likewise served a formal function. Its seating arrangements signified the family's hierarchy; the two heads of table had more comfortable chairs than the ones alongside. In Victorian England and later in North America, the well-to-do could afford a cook and a butler who served meals in well-appointed rooms that boasted elaborate ceiling edges, expensive furnishings, china cabinets, and chandeliers hanging over a large table.

The transition to a less formal arrangement took place half a century ago in small postwar homes. Instead of a dining room builders created a dining space, an area adjacent to the kitchen that was a step up from eating in the kitchen itself. Formality was reinstituted in the 1960s when the overall area of homes increased and a separate dining room started showing up in new houses destined for middle-income homebuyers. This evolution was supported by demographic trends. By the 1960s the early baby boomers had grown up to become adolescents. Family dinners provided an important social function, creating a formal setting for family exchange, reflection on the day's events, and a forum for a get-together. More than a room to house the table and chairs, the dining room became a bonding place. Families would discuss, often debate (this being the sixties), important matters before Dad handed over the car keys to a teenager of driving age after dessert. In large family gatherings, guests would continue to sit long after dinner ended to talk, giggle over photos, or simply catch up with the events of each other's lives.

The mid-1980s saw families and lifestyles transform. Households became smaller and children grew up. Some migrated to follow job opportunities. It became hard to fill up all the empty chairs around the table, and thus the dining room's decline began once again. Its former glory was restored only a few times a year, its charm being revisited on Thanksgiving, Christmas, and other special occasions.

In many homes today the dining room has taken on new roles: kids use the large table surface to do homework; Mom or Dad sets up a computer in a corner to run a freelance business out of home; receipts and bills litter the table at tax time. With the increase in the number and nature of tasks that a modern family has to perform, the dining room often becomes, at least temporarily, a substitute for a study.

The living room experienced a similar fate with the rise of informality. A regular weekday or weekend visit by extended family or acquaintances became a rarity. As the price of sound systems and televisions went down they appeared in several rooms, and no longer did the family need to gather in the living room for entertainment. Central heating eliminated the need for the warmth of fireplaces, and lighting them became time consuming when early wake-ups for work were scheduled for the next day.

Living and dining rooms play an important role in the lives of residents. They always have been and still are as much social and cultural icons as they are functional spaces. As my conversation with Jack the builder demonstrated, the social perception of and economic justification for a formal living or dining space is undergoing a re-evaluation. But as current lifestyle trends result in greater family seclusion, it's important to have uniting symbols.

The dining room represents such a space. Whether it's once a week or several times a year, eating there can put people into a festive mood. Wearing our Sunday best and eating comfort food off the "good" dishes in a formal setting constitute a ritual we should not abandon. On special occasions and holidays it's the room where relatives from near and far congregate. Like the best suits we don for special occasions and jewelry we wear once or twice a year, the dining room is a space to keep. And even when it's not being used, the formal setting, with the table in the middle and chairs all around, sends a clear message about the institution of family.

The living room should continue to play a similar role. After-dinner conversations in a relaxed setting, sitting on an armchair or a sofa while listening to quiet background music, is a sign of civility we seem to have lost. Both living and dining rooms can be the bonding agents of small or even extended families. The spaces could be transformed, perhaps, but their original purpose should remain intact: comfortable rooms that provide a transition between the world outside and within.

Back at the office, I unrolled my drawings again and thought about what Jack had said. I saw his point: too large a home would be too expensive and wouldn't sell. So I decided to shrink all the space equally but keep, albeit transformed, the living and dining rooms. Luckily, he saw my point.

# A CONVERSATION WITH YOUR FRIDGE

THE KITCHEN APPLIANCE SECTION AT THE DALLAS HOME SHOW looked like the set for a Hollywood space voyage movie. Major appliance manufacturers had constructed full-size kitchens in the vast hall with theater-like spotlights shining above. Crowds gathered to watch celebrity chefs slicing vegetables at an enormous speed, nearly missing their fingertips, and pausing from time to time to extol the wonders of the gadgets surrounding them. The shiny stainless-steel appliances with digital readouts were clearly the stars of the display.

You could tell that a lot was at stake. Sales representatives of Whirlpool, Maytag, GE, and Amana carefully monitored the audience, eager to answer questions, wanting to know how impressed people were. Appliance manufacturing has become big business in North America, and the Dallas show, part of the National Association of Home Builders' annual meeting, is where the newer gadgets, just off the drawing board, are paraded. Topping last year's sales mark with new wizardry that will edge out the competition is the goal.

The sales reps in Dallas also know what every builder and real estate agent will confirm: kitchens are a house's number one sales clincher. Appliances, of course, are integral to the kitchen, and featuring the latest ones in a model house will automatically render that house trendy.

The expanding size of kitchens and the monetary investment in their contents stand in marked contrast to their place in the past. How has the kitchen gradually become the home's hub? Why do people invest so much in them and what do appliances have to do with it? And what other ideas are being cooked up by wizards at General Electric and Whirlpool that will make us remodel kitchens and replace perfectly functioning appliances with newer models?

From its humble beginning, the kitchen has maintained its critical importance to home life. Whether the home is small or large, in a city or a rural area, for the wealthy or the poor, the need to store, prepare, and serve three meals a day makes the kitchen an ever-utilitarian place. No wonder, then, that domestic technology innovations were first introduced in the kitchen. It's also the space that was most influenced by the change in the status of women in the household and society.

No generalization can be made about size, form, or location of the kitchen. Yet in single-family houses they were commonly placed at the periphery, adjacent to an exterior wall and a window—a source of natural light and fresh air. Kitchens in older homes were also located in the cellar. In the early colonists' one-room house, in addition to cooking, the wood-burning stove (the only appliance) served as the home's heater on wintry nights. Beds were set around it with the parents in charge of keeping the fire going. Food storage was also a challenging task, and involved root cellars, the salting of meat, and, in the north, refrigeration with blocks of ice. Most of the food had to be prepared daily, taking up a great deal of the homemaker's time. The work itself took place on a table in the center of the kitchen. Water was brought in and stored in a barrel, and dishes were cleaned indoors or outdoors, depending on the season.

The introduction of plumbing, running water, and drainage in the mid-nineteenth century and the development of advanced cooking stoves contributed to a leap forward in the evolution of kitchen technology, design, and functionality. In 1833 Jordan Mott invented the first practical coal stove. He called his invention, which had ventilation to burn the coal efficiently, a base burner. In 1891 the Carpenter Electric Heating Manufacturing Co. invented an electric stove, which was improved and patented in 1896 by William Hadaway. Cooking and washing had developed a fixed place, and an early version of the kitchen layout we know today emerged. The stationary sink, central to food preparation, was placed next to a window so that while meals were prepared toddlers could be watched as they played outside. Along with the permanency of the sink and the stove, storage of dishes, pots, and other cooking utensils was fixed on the wall, first on open shelves and racks and later in cabinets and drawers. The kitchen itself was located in relative proximity to the dining area, separated by a door. Exterior pipes lent the kitchen a rough look and reinforced its image as an annex to the home's other functions. The kitchen was also regarded as the woman's domain—private, and not for everyone to visit.

Food storage changed at the beginning of the nineteenth century with the introduction of canned food and of the icebox. Since the heavy icebox, like the stove and sink, had a fixed location, the three became the kitchen's pivotal anchors. The kitchen layout, as a result, evolved into the one we recognize today.

The invention of the transformer in 1886 by William Stanley (later sold to George Westinghouse), which turned direct current into alternating current, represented another stepping stone in the domestic environment. By allowing electricity to travel between a remote generator and a private residence, the transformer rendered such traditional chores as refilling the icebox obsolete and introduced new ones, further reshaping the kitchen's look and functionality. It's still arguable whether electrical appliances have made the work easier, but they have no doubt reduced some of the labor-intensive chores like dishwashing.

With the soaring popularity of electric appliances came the ongoing development of ever-newer models. Each year's fridges or stoves had to be more advanced than the last's. And since appliances quickly became the kitchen's main features, their appearance was also important. Kitchens gradually began to resemble a showcase.

Parallel to the introduction of electrical appliances, the location of the kitchen in the dwelling and its importance in home life began to change. The small postwar home saw a gradual dismantling of the wall between the kitchen and the dining room. In apartments, the kitchen, dining room, and living spaces were all combined. Appliances were integrated with kitchen cabinets, forming a coherent, functional unit. The countertop was increasingly favored over the table as a place for food preparation, since it was now a resting area for other small-sized appliances. Food mixers, toasters, electric can openers, and the like had a permanent location there. Since more electric power was needed for stoves, fridges, and other appliances, more outlets were introduced on the splash wall between the lower and upper cabinets. Industrial designers were now employed by manufacturers who recognized that form is as important as function. Appliances had to have curb appeal.

The return of women to the labor force en masse in the 1960s and 1970s was another landmark in the evolution of kitchens. The need to wake up toddlers at dawn, feed them quickly while packing lunches, and make it to the carpool and to work on time demanded regimented efficiency. A well-designed kitchen, reliable appliances, stocked cupboards, and a freezer became allies to working parents. Dinnertime was no different. The time it took to make meals, clean, oversee kids' homework, do laundry, and prepare for tomorrow's work day had to be compressed. And with several family members needing to partake in household chores, people became more and more reliant on domestic appliances.

This hectic lifestyle wasn't lost on the appliance manufacturers, nor on the food industry. Burgeoning frozen food sections and the birth of the mega-food chains were testaments to the fact that North American households had shifted to convenience food. A recent *Newsweek* article reported some startling statistics: a mere third of all dinner entrees today are entirely homemade; fully 47 percent of all suppers eaten at home do not involve turning on the oven at all; and the area in supermarkets dedicated to prepared dinners has increased by 168 percent since 1993. Few peel tomatoes to make Grandma's lasagna; instead we thaw a frozen meal and serve it in minutes. Even that American icon, the burger, is now sold frozen in a bun with condiments. Large, once-a-week shopping for convenient, ready-to-serve food has also expanded pantry space. Frozen-food storage has required larger fridges, and even a separate freezer in the basement has been added for long-term storage. Meanwhile, the real kitchens where food is actually prepared have gradually moved to an efficient plant somewhere in the industrial part of town.

The ready-to-serve frozen food benefited from the invention of another appliance: the microwave oven. It was invented in 1946 by accident when Dr. Percy Spencer, an American, tested a radar-related tube called a magnetron. During one of the experiments, a candy bar in his pocket melted. Further testing made him realize the significance of his invention. He fed electrically created microwaves into a metal box, generating a high-density electromagnetic field. When food was placed in the box and microwave energy fed in, the temperature of the food rose rapidly. It was a time-saving leap forward: a frozen item no longer had to be thawed on the counter for hours; it could now be served in minutes. The microwave oven rapidly took center stage in the family's daily kitchen routines. It gradually moved from its early location—on a stand in the kitchen corner—to the countertop, and was quickly placed among the kitchen's top cabinets. Newer models were installed above the stovetop and combined with a fan to draw out odors. The separation between the stovetop and the microwave meant even greater flexibility.

The arrival of the baby boom cohort to the housing market in the 1980s saw the demand for homes further exceed supply. Boomers were eager to spend on comforts, and kitchen appliances were part of this trend. Homeowners turned the kitchen into a house showpiece equivalent to the manicured front lawn. An island was added with a Jenn-Air broiling top for indoor barbecues. A second service sink was introduced, as well as a barlike seating arrangement and a breakfast area. Illuminating these appliances and countertops efficiently and dramatically became part of the overall decor.

With living rooms and dining rooms becoming less important, the kitchen has become the home's social space. The open plan concept has taken on a new meaning, turning the entire floor, or most of it, into one large area, with several functions feeding into the kitchen. Kids' homework, home accounting, reading, watching TV, and entertaining friends all take place in this once-humble space. Kitchens have also annexed adjacent rooms. Kitchen–family room, kitchen–media room, and kitchen–home office are some of the popular layouts. Ironically, the preferred twenty-first-century home layout mirrors that of the early settlers starting their life on this continent—the one-room house.

Turning the kitchen into the family's social center necessitated further upgrades in appearance. Manufacturers, once again, didn't miss a beat. They paid more attention to form and design, calling in top industrial designers to turn bulky appliances into design masterpieces. Clad in stainless steel facings, black edges, and digital readouts, appliances took on a slick personality.

The Sub-Zero company moved the fridge motor to the top, which helped narrow it and make it look like part of the cabinets, and a bottom freezer was introduced. A programmable oven-fridge catered to the needs of households on the move, keeping dinners cool until it's time to start cooking and the food warm until the family arrives before dinnertime. Warmer dish drawers were also developed for those who like to have their favorite recipes served on a hot plate.

Despite a reliance on ready-to-serve meals, homeowners have been willing to pay for the ability to prepare gourmet dinners at home on special occasions. Men have also gotten involved in cooking and are willing to invest in such luxury accessories as a built-in cooler that chills wine to the right temperature and a built-in espresso machine for lattes before a hectic day begins.

A dual dishwasher has eliminated the need to place the dishes back in the cabinet—one compartment washes while the other stores—and in a dual-compartment oven two items can be cooked at different temperatures simultaneously. And with the kitchen now the family gathering and conversation center, quiet appliances have become a must. Noiseless fans and dishwashers are currently on the menu. But perhaps the strangest is yet to come.

Those printed bar codes on food packaging have inspired Whirlpool appliance designers to create a scanning device on the fridge. Upon return with a load of groceries, the shopper will use the device to record products before putting them in the fridge. Future dinner preparations, manufacturers proclaim, will start at work. From your office computer you'll log on to the fridge, find out what it's short of, and so be reminded to stop at the store on the way home. Once at home, a touch-pad screen on the fridge door will offer favorite dinner menus in a soft voice. The recipe and required ingredients are displayed on the screen, along with a step-by-step cooking presentation. And where will the cooking actually take place? In the sink.

The fact that the sink is where the water tap and drain are located is about to lead to the next step in the evolution of cooking. No longer will homeowners have to carry a pot of water to the stove and then carry it back to the sink to drain the hot water from the pasta. The task will begin and end at the sink. Boiling water will steam vegetables and rice, then press a button and the pot will drain directly into the sink.

Blame it on lifestyle, technology, or plain consumerism, but society has changed and people's eating habits have changed as well. Many have gradually disengaged from cooking their own food, the most human and potentially rewarding of tasks. We've adopted a culture of outsourcing, where snow is cleared by subcontractors, gardens looked after by gardeners, and clothing laundered by drycleaners. As far as the kitchen is concerned, if present trends continue, homes will be filled with costly appliances while we watch real cooking on the Food Channel.

# OVERSIZED FURNITURE OR SMALL ROOMS?

I WAS INVITED BY FRIENDS—YOUNG PARENTS OF TWO TODDLERS— to visit their newly acquired home. Located in an established suburb near Montreal, the thirty-five-year-old, 1,500-square-foot (140-square-meter) house was identical to the other ones on the street. The split-level bungalow had a basement parking garage on one side and an elevated living area on the other. As I walked in, my hosts suggested that we tour the house in which they had invested the better part of their savings.

The main level was raised a few steps above the entrance. On the right was the living room. A large, L-shaped, fabric-upholstered sofa filled up most of it. A big square coffee table stood in the center of the space. A 10-foot (3-meter) long shelving unit against the wall held a 42-inch TV set and other electronic accessories in the middle. The other shelves had books and a glass-enclosed display of mementos. Two small speakers rested on white pedestals in the room's corners. An overstuffed armchair stood beside the coffee table and closed the square.

The dining room was an extension of the living area. The redwood table that filled up the space had six chairs, and my hosts explained that it could be extended to seat four more people. A 4-foot (1.2-meter) wide china cabinet with glass doors, part of the set, stood in one of the corners. The dining room was off the kitchen where the breakfast area was located. The main bathroom was wedged between the day and the night zones of the house. A king-sized bed occupied most of the space in the master bedroom, with night tables on each side. In front of the bed was a matching makeup table with a large mirror. The dresser underneath the window that looked onto the backyard was also part of the set.

There were two other smaller bedrooms. One had a young person's bed, a desk, and a toy chest; the one next door had a rocking chair and toys mounted on top of the crib. The lower level had a family room containing another unit with a 60-inch TV set. Here, too, toys were spread all around the carpeted floor. The lower level also had a study with a desk and filing cabinet, and a utility room where the heating system stood. The garage occupied the rest of the floor.

As we made our way back to the upper level I peeked into the bedrooms again. There was nothing outstanding about the home's layout, but I was puzzled by the room sizes. At first glance, they seemed tiny. But then I realized that they weren't small at all. The large dimensions of the furniture distorted the rooms' proportions, making them look less than adequate. The furniture, however, was of the size, type, and design that one finds in most North American furniture or department stores. Was it oversized, or was it just that my friends' house was small?

I am, I have to confess, a minimalist. I do not like cluttered places. Darker walls and poorly lit rooms with heavy curtains are not to my liking. I like free space around furniture and believe that the architecture needs to be appreciated as much as the decor. So why do North American homes often look as if their owners had stuffed them to the brim? The logical response is that we tend to consume more goods and are reluctant to rid ourselves of old stuff. Homeowners, however, simply have no choice. A visit to many furniture stores reveals that much of the available furniture is bulky and poorly designed. It even makes you think that furniture size drives home size.

In the past half-century homes have doubled, and in most markets even tripled, in area. There have been more rooms to furnish in newer designs, and the room area itself has grown. Back in the postwar era designers of small homes paid careful attention to making efficient use of space. Innovative furniture designs were introduced to make do with small bedrooms and kitchens. Storage of bedding accessories, for example, was made part of the bed. In present-day designs, however, squeezing everything in is less of a concern. There's plenty of space in rooms to include any furniture size.

At the turn of the twentieth century Victorian parlors, dining rooms, and kitchens were clearly defined and enclosed by walls. Since then, home design has gradually done away with some of the walls and embraced the open concept. As in my hosts' home, the living and dining areas became a single spatial unit.

In other homes the wall between the kitchen and the dining area or a family room has been removed. The airy arrangement helps make rooms look less cluttered with oversized furniture in them.

New lifestyle trends and habits have had another significant impact on the design and consumption of furnishings. The home theater, with a giant TV and surround-sound speaker system, has become a common feature of living or family rooms. Comfortable seating arrangements have consequently grown in demand: viewers want to rest their entire body on the sofa, or, at the very least, their legs on the coffee table, and they need more surfaces for snacks while they're watching TV. The introduction of TVs and stereos to kids' rooms, master bedrooms, and kitchens has also meant the need for comfortable arrangements. And with the need to accommodate a computer, monitor, printer, and scanner, multi-shelf desk systems have started to appear, further increasing the demand for space.

The marketing of furniture has also contributed to over-consumption and to the cluttering of North American homes. Rather than choose individual items, people have responded favorably to offers to buy an entire matching set for a room. A living room package typically includes sofas, a coffee table, and a wall unit. Dining sets comprise tables and chairs and a china cabinet, and a master bedroom set includes a bed, night tables, a dresser, and a makeup counter. And since a package represents a "deal," homeowners are tempted to buy all the set's pieces whether they need them or not. Unsurprisingly, once a house is furnished in this way, people often begin to think about moving to a larger one.

With so few North American furnishing stores catering to the needs of small-home or apartment dwellers, foreign chain stores such as Ikea, Caban, and Fly have attracted a wide range of loyal customers with their small-size furnishings and accessories. European designs also have a grace and style that North American designs often lack. Having had to cope through generations with the constraints of high-density apartment living, Europeans have developed furnishings that are masterpieces of beauty and compact functionality. Top manufacturers employ talented designers who create large numbers of prototypes until a display model is chosen and mass-produced. A visit to the Fiera di Milano, Europe's largest design show, is a breathtaking experience. Furniture is regarded as artwork, and acclaimed designers are featured and rewarded.

The craftsmanship of North American furniture, in contrast, has gone down in recent years. Mechanized production systems and cheaper, synthetic materials have reduced furniture's durability and eliminated our nostalgic, long-lasting attachment to favored pieces. Close inspection of a bureau, for example, reveals that the visible outer components are made of plywood covered with a thin veneer layer. The drawers themselves are often made of plastics or medium-density fiber, with the bottoms made of masonite. Components are attached not with traditional woodworking joints but with nail guns or glue. This is a far cry from the way chairs and cabinets used to be constructed and from the materials that were once used to build them. Upmarket furnishings, surprisingly, are no different. The facing material is perhaps more expensive—like teak or mahogany—but the craftsmanship is often just as poor. Customers rarely have a choice in the matter, since old-fashioned, properly built pieces are hard to find.

Cheaper, do-it-yourself furnishings have also become highly popular in recent years. The products are designed with simplicity of assembly in mind and in most cases have a limited life. No one plans to bequeath to their sons and daughters a piece of furniture bought at a furniture mart.

Ironically, public craving for old-style furniture has grown, as attested by the proliferation of antique stores in many towns. People flock to these stores, ready to pay for the warmth and charm that old pieces hold. Underneath it all, perhaps, is their desire to buy a slice of history. An old redwood dining room table with its scratches and markings can be a reminder of the lives lived around it over the years. A hand-carved armoire inherited from Grandma is more than a storage place for dishes; it's a part of family history that can be passed on to future generations one day.

Consumers have become more educated these days and have developed sophisticated taste. Travel abroad, interior design magazines, and TV shows have all exposed homeowners to small, well-crafted furniture. Manufacturers will, one hopes, follow the trend and expand their offerings to combine size, function, and beauty.

# TIMELESS DESIGN

THE WOMAN WHO STOOD ON OUR FRONT PORCH LOOKED TIMID. She introduced herself and said that she'd lived in our house when she was a child. She lived in the United States now, she went on, and was in town for a family gathering.

It was a hot August day, the trees overhead in full bloom. The woman seemed to be in her mid-sixties, and since our house was built in the early 1930s, I figured she must have lived here shortly after its construction. There was a moment of silence, and then she pointed to Bill's Glass Shop across the street. "That's where Quality Reading used to be," she said. "My mother would stand right here watching me cross the street to exchange books." When I told her that we'd moved in a couple of years earlier, she asked from whom we'd bought the house. I told her about the elderly woman who sold us the duplex and moved upstairs to become our tenant. Her father, she said, had sold the place to a Greek fellow whose name she had forgotten.

She saw the two steps inside our foyer and mentioned that when she was a toddler her mother used to sit her on them and tie her shoelaces. We'd done the same with our kids when they were young, I laughed. I invited her to come in. She walked into the dining room and said "This was my uncle's bedroom when he and his wife immigrated to Canada after the war." She crossed the hallway into our living room, touching the ragged plaster wall and saying that she remembered it painted green. "It was our family room. We did everything here. Our big radio stood in the corner."

"This was my parents' place," she continued when we reached the master bedroom. "There were two closets against this wall." I told her that we'd found them too small and had decided to replace them with a large built-in. She was surprised to see what we'd done to the bathroom. It was time to replace the old plumbing, I explained. "Where's my favorite breakfast nook?" she asked when we reached the kitchen. I told her that the wall between the nook and the kitchen had been removed by one of the previous owners. "We'd sit right here near a round table and my mom would serve my sister and me breakfast." She showed me where the icebox had been and pointed to the outside windowsill where her mother used to keep the milk in winter. She asked if she could see the small bedroom that she and her sister had shared, and later asked about the basement. As we stepped to the lower level I told her that we'd finished the basement a year ago. It had been her favorite play space, she said, and a noisy oil furnace had kept the place warm in winter. She showed me how the laundry was hung and where the fireplace wood was kept. We walked back up. As we parted she thanked me for inviting her in and said her visit had brought back nice memories.

When she left I thought about how homes are built to last longer than the lives of their occupants. When homes are designed and built they're characterized by the tendencies and technologies of that time, yet in later years the decisions that shaped the original design become increasingly dated. A process of keeping up with change—either in people's lives or in technological innovation—inevitably begins upon occupancy. I wondered whether homes could be designed to facilitate ongoing adaptability. Why, despite the recently introduced building technologies, are people still constrained by permanent walls, unable to relocate them as they do with furniture? I also thought about why people would remodel their places. What triggers such a process? Is it a desire for self-expression, simple functional needs, or a move to a dwelling whose layout was determined by someone else?

Mobility, in fact, is known to be an important consideration in a home's remodeling. North Americans are known to move on average every ten years. New homes are designed to fit the needs of their first occupant, but over time are refitted by subsequent owners to their own needs, habits, and lifestyles. As I had adapted the house I bought from the previous owner, and as she had adapted it from the Greek fellow who bought it from my visitor's father, so future occupants will modify things further.

The Industrial Revolution, which marked a turning point in many urban and societal structures, also marked the start of residential mobility in its present form. People abandoned an agrarian way of life and left land that had been cultivated for generations to seek work in urban centers. They settled where work was available. Homes were no longer the residences of several generations but were bought and sold when circumstances warranted. When homeowners could find better solutions for their space needs in another residence, they traded in their old one.

The end of the Second World War marked another turning point. Society began to undergo an even greater acceleration in the pace of change. Later, the introduction of reliable forms of birth control affected the size of families, and the influential power of the media and consumerism affected their lives at home. Society, it seems, has become accustomed to the fact that constant changes are inevitable. These changes necessitate a new design approach in which future dwellings need to be more adaptable to societal trends and, as a result, their occupants' lives.

There is, in fact, an apparent conflict in homes between the dynamic nature of their residents' lives and the constraints imposed by the permanency of their design. Toddlers, for example, require attention; their rooms need to be located near their parents'. During adolescence they may seek privacy and want their rooms farther away. At times we wish that we could move rooms around like toy blocks. That's not possible, of course, but what about a timeless design, a design that facilitates a better fit between the home and the twists and turns of life?

A stroll through many old neighborhoods in my city, Montreal, reveals that such a design does exist. With its trademark curving stairs that lead into second- and third-floor porches, the plex has displayed a great degree of flexibility over the decades. This housing type is said to have first been built in 1852 by the Grand Trunk Railway Company as workers' housing. One family occupied the duplex's lower floor and another the upper. It was an urban, fairly dense, and above all highly affordable housing solution. Over the ensuing decades, the duplex evolved into a triplex for three families living on top of each other—and even a fourplex when a basement suite was included. Montrealers soon discovered that the concept had economic merit as a rental property; they could live on one floor, usually the lower, and rent out the other two.

But most intriguing was the approach to the plex's interior design. Since the identity and the space needs of future renters were unknown, the dwellings were designed with a generic layout. The floor plan was either a single- or double-loaded corridor. Rooms were often of equal dimensions, permitting their use as bedrooms, living rooms, or dining rooms. The windows were of identical proportions throughout, which did not limit the use of the room to a single function. A door was commonly placed between the front two rooms, letting the occupants turn them into a large single space or keep them apart. The room often functioned as a living–dining combination. Kitchens and bathrooms were placed either at the dark middle area of the floor or at the rear, letting more sunlight into the main front rooms.

Doors to the rooms off the central corridor were placed at the center of the wall, meaning that all the perimeter walls could be used. Some plexes had rooms with no built-in clothes closets, which contributed to their versatility: whereas their early occupants used large dressers as closets instead, contemporary occupants can turn these rooms into something other than bedrooms. Over the past century builders have introduced few changes to this timeless design, and plexes have remained highly popular in Montreal. In fact, many of the old plexes are now eagerly sought after by younger homebuyers who plan to fit their original design to contemporary uses.

Designing for adaptability was also attempted after the Second World War. The return of millions of veterans to North America and the ensuing baby boom of the 1940s and 1950s, coupled with the stagnant state of the housing industry as an after-effect of the Depression years, created a housing crisis of great magnitude. The crisis stimulated builders and designers to look into innovative design and building technologies that resulted in the development of small, affordable, adaptable homes.

Designers modified traditional house planning to accommodate present and future demands of inhabitants. The living room, for example, was expanded to increase its flexibility as an all-purpose space, becoming as well a study, dining room, parlor, and playroom.

The kitchen, no longer relegated to the rear of the house, was integrated into this multifunctional living area. It became a U- or L-shaped workspace equipped with practical appliances. A low counter formed the only division between the kitchen and living area, creating a practical, adaptable, and efficient utility space where parents could watch over children playing and serve meals in the adjacent dining area.

With the scarcity of interior space in postwar homes and the ongoing needs of the family, walls were brought down to improve adaptability. An open floor plan allowed people to define their space according to how they lived. They could easily transform their living spaces with such innovative features as sliding walls and movable partitions, modifying their privacy levels and creating or merging rooms at their discretion.

As North America moved into the prosperous 1950s and 1960s the need for adaptable and expandable housing strategies subsided. Buyers had the means to afford larger homes, and builders were eager to build them. Gradually, expanded lot sizes and higher housing standards eliminated the need to use small spaces efficiently. The building industry fell into a traditional conservative pattern where a limited number of house types were the norm and innovative ideas such as adaptability were regarded as unnecessary frills.

Recent decades have provided ample reasons for greater choice in home design. The new domestic technologies, the rise in nontraditional households, the lengthening of people's lives, and the increasing numbers of those who work at home have all introduced uncommon design challenges.

Consequently, some builders are looking to incorporate greater flexibility in the way homes are sold, built, and used. Enter José Di Bona. The Montreal builder, president of Anobid Construction, believes that houses, just like cars or furniture, can come with options and be sold à la carte. His innovative downtown housing project—comprising eighteen three-story wood-frame townhouses built in a row—caters to an as yet untapped market niche. Di Bona saw the townhouses as a "big volume" to be divided and sold according to his clients' needs and budgets. Each slice of the row was therefore arranged differently inside. A single family bought all three floors of one unit, for example, while two families bought the adjacent unit. Another was bought by a client who lives in the two lower floors and rents out the top one.

Di Bona, whose sales brochure reads like a restaurant menu, sells his houses by the floor. And he believes that new market trends support his approach. The demographic composition of today's family is much more diverse, he explains, especially in urban markets. The downtown area attracts nontraditional households who are tempted by the close proximity to work that enables them to do without a car. They also, he says, have varied lifestyles, and hence differing housing needs.

Carole Fournier and her husband, Di Bona's clients, were attracted by the project's location in the heart of the city. They occupy a three-story unit with their young son. Fournier, a dietitian, uses the ground floor as a home office. The space has a desk and a bookshelf in the front room overlooking the street. It's very convenient, she says, because here her clients need not enter the private area of her house. She's considering renting out the lower level when she and her husband retire.

Di Bona applied the menu principle, which encompasses more options than are normally offered by tract developers, to the interior finishes as well. For an additional $500 buyers can have the plumbing prepared for a future bathroom in the basement, and for $2,400 they can have the entire bathroom built. Di Bona believes that his clientele don't mind paying the administrative fees for coordinating these choices. He may sell a unit to a single person who enjoys cooking and is willing to pay for a large kitchen. Another household, a couple, may prefer to dine out, and so will want a smaller kitchen. Instead, they may want special acoustic wall insulation for their top-of-the-line sound system. Before construction began Di Bona even altered the facade of the building. Those who work at home, he said, wanted larger windows. He won't change the front elevation, but he is flexible about the design of the rear of the building, where zoning bylaws are more lax.

Di Bona's practice is likely to be a mark of things to come. Continued demographic diversity coupled with technological innovation allows builders to give clients a greater variety of design options. Wide-span engineered floor joists have eliminated the need for interior-bearing partitions. Flexible hot and cold tubing means that bathrooms and kitchens can be located anywhere on the floor. These "wet" functions no longer have to be stacked on top of one another, as is common practice in multi-story housing projects.

The use of computers in marketing and sales simplifies the administrative issues in accommodating buyers' choices. On-screen display of alternative floor plans and finishings is becoming common practice. Other software programs allow the builder to readily tally up the cost of the various options chosen by the homeowner. This way, decisions as to what the final package may include can be made quickly.

Constructing a shell and then allowing homebuyers to select options and to participate in the interior design of their dwelling is emerging as the next generation of home design, marketing, and building—and one that will likely continue to evolve.

## HOMES WITH A GLOBAL REACH

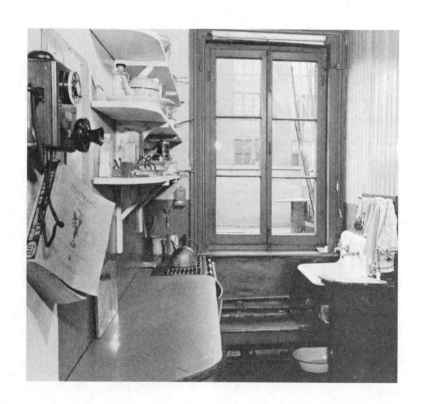

JETLAGGED FROM A RECENT TRIP OVERSEAS, I LAY IN BED TRYING hard to fall asleep. At two in the morning, I watched the numbers on my bedside clock change one by one. I counted all the sheep in the world. I tried to recite a long-forgotten children's song, also to no avail. I was fully awake and staring at the dark ceiling. I knew I'd be in trouble later that morning, with a busy day of work ahead.

It occurred to me that I could begin some of the day's chores rather than wait until the morning. So, I went to my study and turned on the computer. I keyed in my password and logged on to a program that enables me to access my office computer. I checked my email first. Some real messages were nestled in between the spam, and I read and responded to them. A sound alerted me that I had just received mail. It was from a colleague in the country from which I had just returned, inquiring if I'd made it home safely and thanking me for my visit and the lecture I'd given at his university. He asked me to provide him with references to an author I had mentioned in my talk. I surfed the website of my university's library, copied a list of books by the author, and sent it to my colleague. I received his thanks within minutes. Next I did some banking, checking my balances and paying some bills. Then I ordered a recently published book that I'd read about on the plane, and searched for a story in an online newspaper overseas.

Sitting in front of the computer, I thought about the effect it's had on the domestic environment. Computers have expanded the home's time and space, allowing occupants to be anywhere, at any time. They have brought into the home slices of activities that used to be carried out in other places not so long ago. A bank, a library, and a travel agency are some of the institutions that we used to visit in person during daytime hours and that we can now access digitally from home. Computers provide residences with a distant reach. Yet at the same time they've detached us from these places; we no longer need to patronize them in person. Computers have also contributed to segregation within the home itself. Household members of all ages now have a tool that lets them spend less time with each other.

The first appliance to open the home's communication avenue and make this ambivalent contribution to home life was, of course, the telephone. I wondered how the telephone, besides being a technological breakthrough, had affected the layout of the home over the past century. How had it influenced home and community life? Are computers destined to follow the same route, forever making the home dependent on their services? What's next in the relationship between the home and information appliances?

When Alexander Graham Bell patented the telephone in 1876 he altered the nature of human interaction overnight. The ability to reach someone at once and carry on a live conversation over a wire rendered written messages, sent by snail mail, to a certain degree obsolete. Instant communication was born and, along with it, instant exchange of news and ideas. Like other great inventions that preceded and followed it, the telephone was first viewed with skepticism. Early forecasters even argued that it would never take off since its initiators wouldn't be able to find enough single women between the ages of sixteen and twenty to operate the manual switchboards. Only a few envisioned the effect that the telephone would eventually have on home design and life in the following century.

The telephone formulated a new kind of social network. Establishments known to be gathering places for information exchange and gossip began their decline. The town's public square lost its appeal. The telephone even eroded face-to-face interaction among members of an extended family. Large-scale mobility that began with the onset of the Industrial Revolution, coupled with the proliferation of the telephone in later years, enabled families to maintain long-distance relationships. People could talk daily with someone from afar.

The residential street too was transformed. Whereas the front porch had served as an instrument of social contact, chatting with passersby and gathering communal news became less necessary when you could talk on the phone with the neighbor next door or across the street. The telephone also marked the beginning of that blurring of the line between home and work in the modern era. Years later, as services expanded, the same lines were used for homes and businesses, allowing people at home to receive after-hours calls directed to their stores or offices.

When it was first introduced the telephone was placed in the hallway or the living room, closer to the entrance. Given its sporadic use, it was initially enclosed within a cabinet. Only years later would it be hung on the wall and, later still, stand alone. The ring of a telephone disturbed routine family activities and attracted immediate attention. People would gather around to find out who called and what the message was. Party lines enabled people to listen to their neighbors' private conversations.

The evolution in telephone technology and the proliferation of its use were remarkable. In 1881 the Bell Telephone Company reported a 9 percent annual growth in subscription; by 1894 the rate had leapt to 27 percent. User fee rates began to decline: from $150 per 1,000 calls in 1890, the rates dropped to $78 per 1,000 in 1905 and $51 per 1,000 calls in 1915.

Over the following decades, as telephone technology transformed from manual to automated switchboards and hardware and service costs went down, a telephone extension in other rooms appeared. Some people installed a second line, enabling household members, often teenagers, to conduct extended conversations from the privacy of their rooms. With these clear demarcations within the family, phone calls within the home turned from a public into a private affair.

Then in the 1950s the installation of jacks throughout the house enabled people to talk on the phone while preparing dinner, watching TV, or working on a school project. Cordless communication in the 1990s encouraged mobility from room to room and floor to floor. A person could now verify information or check a reference without saying "I'll call you back."

The many other more recent services that telephone companies offer today have made the phone even more convenient and efficient. Messaging systems enable us to receive urgent information, call forwarding to receive a call away from home, call display to screen calls, and teleconferencing and speakerphones to talk to more than two people at a time.

The telephone, of course, introduced us to the ordering-in of goods and services. It also provided a safety net of sorts. Emergency services like medical, police, and fire departments are a phone call away, further expanding a sense of security at home.

Cellular technology widened this convenience, further blurring the line between the home and the outdoors. In our ever-accelerating lifestyles, cellular phones have become a tool of time management and coordination. The use of cellphones is now common throughout the world. According to 2004 statistics provided by Nokia, worldwide shipments of handsets grew 300 percent from 101 million in 1997 to 405 million units in 2002, and have grown significantly thereafter. Instructions can now be sent to and received from anywhere. The whereabouts of a child can be verified at an instant, a missing dinner ingredient can be ordered, text messaging received, information from the net retrieved, and photos taken and sent.

The invention of the telephone and its use at home has generated many advantages and at the same time contributed to societal losses. Computers brought with them the very same ambivalence. Just a few years after their introduction, they had their fingerprints all over the domestic realm. Whereas the telephone was initially envisioned for residential and commercial applications, computers, and later the internet, were originally conceived for military purposes. The first computers were cumbersome, occupied huge spaces, and were used primarily as calculators. Their size and mode of operation made them not even remotely applicable for domestic use. The invention of the transistor by William Shockley, Walter Brattain, and John Bardeen in the late 1940s altered the course of history.

The obsolescence of vacuum tubes, the development of the chip, and the subsequent compression of size did not lead home users to embrace computers instantly. Their full potential was recognized only years later. They were first seen as hobby instruments, large calculators, a new brand of typewriters, or expensive toys. It was only with the introduction of the internet and its widespread use that a mass revolution began and the home got connected to yet another communication device.

Computers have become a highly interactive mode of communication whose full potential has yet to be exploited. More than a technological and communication breakthrough, the computer is on the leading edge of a knowledge revolution. From the comfort of the domestic sphere it permits access to huge stockpiles of data at an enormous speed. Computers have also become catchall appliances combining telegraph, telephone, radio, television, and typewriter. Later evolution saw them becoming film studios, editing devices, and sophisticated graphic design and printing machines. They've become an integral part of a modern domestic environment without which many everyday chores would be hard to accomplish. The need to provide each family member with his or her own computer, and the never-ending need to keep up with their advancements, have contributed to an accelerated consumption. A household must have at least one, preferably the latest model, if its members wish to be part of the wired community.

The location of computers in homes has changed along with their increasing importance. They were first put in the basement when they were used for hobby or play, moved to the study when they became a sophisticated typewriter, and relocated again to the children's bedroom desk when they became more versatile. They turned mobile with the production of the laptop. U.S. Census Bureau data shows that in 2001 56.5 percent of U.S. households had computers, more than 35 percent of which are estimated to be laptops. This number has grown significantly since.

If the telephone reduced the need for face-to-face contact and contributed to the erosion of the front porch, the computer became the porch. By the year 2001, 50.5 percent of all U.S. households had internet access. Talking with someone online didn't replace the telephone; it added another dimension to it. Chat rooms and dating services became a tool for forming relationships between people who've never met before. Computers also brought the office right into the home. Many found it convenient and economically rewarding to work from home, saving on transportation time and office rental expenses. In 1994 there were 7.6 million home-based workers in the U.S. According to the U.S. Bureau of Labor Statistics, the number rose to 19.8 million in the year 2001.

Unlike the simplicity and ease of operating a telephone, use of computers requires specialized skills and typing proficiency. Younger generations use computers more widely than older people, the digital divide separating those who've embraced the technology from those who've had difficulty adapting to it. It's become a tool predominantly for the younger generations.

The late 1990s was a time of great speculation about the relationship between the home and its environment in the digital age. The term *cocooning* had become familiar, forecasting that in the not-too-distant future, relationships between the home and outside services would be handled mainly by computers. The dot-com companies, some with hardly any activity, product, or economic justification, flourished. The term *convergence* was also widely cited by the public and investors, marking an era of mergers between information generators and information providers. The internet was regarded as tomorrow's generator of new capital, just as the railways and oil were at the turn of the century.

The hype, of course, came to a screeching halt a few years later. Forecasts turned out to be exaggerated and many of the mergers came undone. Yet the basic infrastructure links between homes and servers remained intact. By then most homes were connected to the internet and users were going online daily. According to the CIA *World Factbook,* in the year 2002, 16.11 million Canadians had internet access at home.

Current trends can forecast those services that internet home users will come to rely on. Shopping for some goods and services online will be one of them. The simplicity associated with online travel services, banking, ticket reservations, and the buying of products not available in stores next door means that they'll likely continue to flourish. Main Street and the shopping mall won't vanish, though; people still like to visit, to see and feel products, to buy them in person. And finally, with Digital Versatile Disc readers having turned computers into television monitors, entertainment will be another service whose distribution online is bound only to expand, along with other entertainment services on demand.

The third area of growth is likely to be monitoring and consultation services in the medical field. With the graying of North America and as more people are expected to seek medical assistance, health-care costs are expected to rise. A patient is already able to chat with a health-care specialist using a computer equipped with a built-in two-way camera and gadgets that check and transmit vital signs to a medical clinic for record-keeping. People won't likely stop visiting medical clinics, yet their computer can become their first line of consultation.

Like the telephone, computers have contributed to decentralized relationships among household members. People are now required to spend more time with them for everyday chores. Much as I did upon returning from my trip overseas, they permit us to put in additional working hours from home, further reducing the time we devote to family relationships.

Just as computer hardware is constantly changing, computer use at home continues to evolve. Communication devices like the telephone and computer have transformed both the relationship that a dwelling has with its near and far environments and the relationships among household members who live together under one roof.

THERE GOES THE NEIGHBORHOOD

# LIVING ABOVE THE STORE

I WALKED THE STREETS AND ALLEYWAYS OF ISTANBUL ON A HOT June day. The heart of this Turkish city of twelve million on the Bosphorus Straits, spanning two continents and home to Hagia Sophia and the Blue Mosque, is a crowded place. From the Blue Mosque I headed along Babiali Cad street to the Spice Bazaar. Oriental food displays and aromas drew lunch-hour patrons into the restaurants. The narrow streets funneled into a large open square in front of Yeni Cami Mosque. The blue water of the Sea of Marmara was on my far right with tour boats docking in the nearby port.

The crowd grew denser as I walked into the square. In the distance I saw the bazaar's gate. I bought a slice of chilled watermelon and stood in the shade of the stand's umbrella as vendors carrying cigarettes, toys, and candy walked by announcing their merchandise. The noise grew louder as I entered the bazaar. The buildings' side walls were dirty and the plaster was peeling off some of them. I couldn't avoid the throngs of people filling the narrow street, and elbowed my way through.

During the Byzantine period the bazaar was a place to which merchants from Genoa and Venice came to exchange goods. The trading of Near and Far East spices and medicine lent the place its name. The bazaar's buildings were completed in the second half of the seventeenth century, and since then a multitude of daily visitors, both local and foreign, have witnessed its vitality.

Boxes packed with colorful, strongly scented spices were neatly laid out in front of some stores. Lukum, Turkish delight, was sold in the store next door, and bars of soap in the next. The smells blended with one another, creating a unique aroma. I walked slowly from shop to shop, admiring the goods and savoring the sweets handed to me by an eager merchant. At the end of the bazaar I began walking along a narrow street with a mix of stores and stands at the ground level of a four-story cinderblock walk-up. The apartments' balconies were packed with household goods; some had laundry hanging there. Elderly people sat quietly in others, watching the commotion below. It was past lunch hour now, and kids started to fill up the street for playtime.

Standing there, looking back toward the bazaar's exit and to the balconies above, I wondered about the mix. Behind me was one of the most recognized places in the Near East, a veritable cartel of trade in the heart of a residential district. I was fascinated by the layering: commerce on the ground, with its noise and smells, and daily household routine above. It looked well-suited and natural.

When I further reflected on the bazaar I realized that it was, in fact, a mall, the forerunner of our North American icon. The bustling square at the edge of the covered street, the nearby mosque, and the port were among the anchors that drew crowds to the area. Once they arrived, patrons walked in a covered street, shopping on each side. The marked difference between Istanbul and North American cities was the mall's location. Eastern cities are organic. Activities, uses, and people are mixed together, and living next to or above a store is common. Why, then, hasn't such a model evolved in North America? When did our neighborhoods begin to separate residential from commercial activities? Why do we need to rely on the car for basic household necessities like bread and milk, and why do we resist building stores in new developments? Will mixed-use developments ever be built in suburban towns? Is living above the store going to be an option here at all?

North American cities and small towns initially evolved just the same as their Eastern counterparts until, in the 1920s, they began to segregate uses. The quest for alternatives to downtown shopping was behind the introduction of the mall. In 1923 the J.C. Nichols' Company opened the Country Club Plaza Shopping Center in Kansas City. Several buildings were constructed, with stores on the lower floor and professional offices on the upper. The newness of the idea caught people's attention, but it was never considered a threat to urban commercial activities since few people owned a car in small-town America and ideas were slow to spread. In the 1930s the continent was in the grip of the Depression, and frugality ruled. That all began to change in the postwar era. The transformation of the North American landscape, the birth of suburbia, the proliferation of the private motor vehicle, and the emergence of consumption as the driving force behind the country's prosperity all set the stage for the rise of the shopping mall.

Early suburban planning was designed to alleviate the misery of urban dwellers. In 1816 Robert Owen, an Englishman, proposed New Lanark, a reputable square module where approximately 1,200 people could live. Owen envisioned an enclosed public square that would contain communal and recreational buildings. It was, in other words, an integrated arrangement.

Abandoning overly crowded cities was also at the heart of the postwar urban evolution. The model that North American developers created in the 1950s, however, was segregated. Work and shopping were seen as separate from living, and were placed apart. Developers also capitalized on the fact that land could now be sold for residential uses at one price and at a much higher one for commercial development. The rental income from these businesses could generate the cash flow to spawn more such developments. Getting people to the mall was no longer a concern. Settling in the burbs required each household to own at least one car. Surrounding shopping malls with enough parking for the busiest shopping day of the year, the Saturday before Christmas Eve, was essential. The first enclosed mall, called Southdale, opened in Edina, Minnesota, in 1956. In some communities, malls with restaurants and cinemas became social centers and meeting places. Mom-and-Pop stores in the older parts of town didn't stand a chance against malls, and Main Street began its inevitable decline.

Low-density residential developments just didn't have the economy of scale needed for the co-existence of commerce. Driving to buy every daily household necessity became common, a walk to the corner store a thing of the past. In their book *Sustainable Communities,* Sim Van Der Ryn and Peter Calthorp suggest that approximately 20 percent of all car trips in surburbia are shopping related. Meeting an acquaintance on the street or in a corner store, integral to successful community life, has been replaced by meeting someone at the mall or mall-walking among seniors.

Mall developers operate with a different set of motives in mind. Fitting the building to a local architectural context and contributing to the social welfare of a community aren't their priorities; rather, conceiving designs that will draw in more people and encourage them to shop is the goal. The building itself is meant to last long enough to generate return on investment and maximize profit. Cascading water, Muzak, indoor gardens, and toddlers' play areas are some of the attractions that have drawn people to malls over the years. And when a new shopping place springs up next door the old establishment closes, leaving an urban scar for all to see.

Over the past half-century, suburban commercial development has evolved from the shopping strip to the shopping mall, which has in turn been threatened by the big box concept. Whereas the covered mall provides an enclosed space for people to meet, the big box store has turned shopping into a highly efficient and profitable venture. Customers park their vehicles right in front, buy, and leave. The stores themselves resemble warehouses, utilitarian and simple in form. The mall's indoor walking street stretching between the main anchors is gone. Seen from above, the vast expanses of roofs and parking dominate the landscape. Building a residential floor above the stores is prohibited, local zoning having ensured that residential and commercial uses don't mix. When asked why, officials tend to respond that no one would want to live there anyway.

There are a few exceptions, however; and some, small in scale as they might be, can serve as models for future developments. A while ago I walked into Aubé Frères, a clothing store on Pitt Street in Cornwall, Ontario. The two-story brick building has a row of stores at street level and an office floor above. Its owner, Connie Aubé, told me that he's had his store on that street since 1972. When I asked him where he lived, he pointed up and offered to show me his home. He pushed the metal door open and we stepped out into a sunny afternoon and the row of parked cars ahead. "There it is," he announced. I turned around and saw a single-story house on the roof. It looked as if someone had landed a bungalow from above. It had all the domestic markings: pitched roof, gray painted wood siding, large picture windows, and flower boxes with red geraniums in front.

Connie watched my amazement and suggested we go up. As we climbed he told me that he and his late wife had decided to build the house when they got tired of driving from their suburban cottage to town and back every day. We reached the landing at the top of the stairs. The house, recessed a bit from the back wall, even had a front yard. Two lawn chairs and a garden umbrella gave the place a backyard feel. "Here on the patio I spend evenings reading my paper and listening to music," he told me.

We entered the house. The tastefully decorated living room off the main door had wood flooring and a fireplace. The open kitchen and the dining area occupied the center of the 1,360-square-foot (126-square-meter) house, with a large skylight above the dining table drawing sun into the space. Farther back was a utility room, a bathroom, and a large bedroom at the rear that was, in fact, the front of the building on top of which the house was built. The back wall was recessed a bit, but I could still see the action on Pitt Street below. What about the noise? I asked. "Nothing to disturb my sleep," Connie answered. "Besides, after a while I got used to it."

I tried to figure out how to define what I saw. It wasn't a loft, nor an upward addition: it was, simply, a single-family house on the roof. I asked Connie if he'd had difficulty obtaining a city permit. "Not really," he said. "I engaged an engineer who studied the existing structure and confirmed that it could support a house. Then I had floor plans prepared. We respected height restrictions and local bylaws and codes." As I glanced again to Pitt Street I mulled over what I had just seen. With persistent calls to curb suburban sprawl, Connie's home made a lot of sense. Densifying existing urban settings has emerged as the only remedy to suburban sprawl and diminishing amounts of forested and agricultural land. Living above the store is an old idea, but why not let people add a story to buildings with flat roofs that can support such a load? Homes on the roof may not seem so strange after all if appropriate bylaws are put in place.

Single-use zoning is common in most of North American suburban towns; the bylaws clearly prohibit commercial activities of any kind. There's even a false notion that living around the corner from a grocery store lowers the value of residential properties. Across the street from where I live are a stained-glass artisan store, a bicycle repair shop, and a barber, all on the ground level of an apartment block. I thoroughly enjoy their presence and often get into conversations with Bill, who owns the glass store, and Steve, my barber, and it's nice to watch the kids gather around the bike shop to check out the new models. There's hardly any noise, and the shopkeepers understand that their success and acceptance in the neighborhood depend on their contributing to it, despite the fact that they may live elsewhere.

North America has undergone fundamental changes that make it necessary to re-evaluate archaic bylaws. Driven by the information revolution, homes can be places for more than one activity. Fax and email have enabled people to run a business from home without anyone noticing. Professionals such as translators, illustrators, and bookkeepers are running their businesses from the heart of many suburban neighborhoods. But according to current bylaws, it's hard to determine whether their activities are legal or not.

Other activities can also be introduced into the residential environment. What about a hairdresser, a dental clinic, or a small bookstore? Such services currently occupy the lower levels of condominium towers in many cities, and they could become part of the ground floor of suburban houses as well. How about allowing the conversion of an unused back shed into an artisan's workshop? Suggestions like these send shivers up the spines of many zoning officials, who foresee backed-up traffic and parking problems. I don't believe that such a risk is real. Current parking regulations in most suburban locations already require homeowners to park cars indoors or in driveways. During the daytime the streets in suburbia are often empty anyway. And then there's the myth of excess garbage and the overloading of the infrastructure: once again, none of these claims has ever been proven. For the most part, infrastructure in new and even older communities is oversized.

I can only hope that suburban legislators' mindset will change, and that stores will pop up on the lower level of suburban homes or on a street intersection sometime soon. It's also possible that home offices will become a legal, permanent fixture in other neighborhoods. Living above a business can become part of the charm of new North American communities, and not only for cities such as Istanbul.

# DESIGNING FOR CIVILITY

WHEN MY CHILDREN WERE GROWING UP I LOOKED FORWARD TO accompanying them on Halloween nights. Being an immigrant to Canada, the night's customs were new to me. I kept a watchful eye on my kids as they crossed streets to trick-or-treat, and was particularly amused with the transformation of my neighbors' front lawns. I admired their efforts in making the night festive. Fake body parts stuck out of the ground at one home; ghostly figures hung from trees in another. There were special lights and sound effects to grab youngsters' attention, and magnificent displays of carved pumpkins with flickering candles inside. I always wondered why my neighbors invested so much effort in a holiday that lasts so short a time. My intuitive answer was tradition. Parents who once trick-or-treated wanted their own kids to have the same unforgettable experience. But after further thought, I realized that what they were really doing was reinforcing the bonds of community.

I live in one of Montreal's oldest neighborhoods, called Notre-Dame-de-Grâce. Montrealers refer to it as NDG. It has the markings of a place that has matured gracefully over the years. It began in the early 1800s as an agricultural settlement, home to farmers and several well-off families who maintained residences in town. In 1920 the village was annexed by the City of Montreal, and the wheels of its suburban development were set in motion. Electric tramlines were extended and the pleasant area quickly attracted city dwellers. The population of NDG soared from 5,000 in 1914 to a bustling 50,000 by the 1930s. After the Second World War, the baby boom that swelled suburban populations across North America similarly affected NDG. By the early 1960s its neighborhoods had filled with housing and it began to mature as a complete community. Today 70,000 people call Notre-Dame-de-Grâce home.

The houses on my street are all semi-detached duplexes, with owners occupying the main floor and basement and tenants the upper level. The brick-clad homes have aged over time: their well-tended front lawns, painted wooden porches, metal railings on balconies, and stained-glass windows on front-door transoms and windows are some of the touches that lend them their charm. The trees have grown to form a green canopy over streets and backyards in summer and become beautiful scenery when covered in snow in winter. Neighborhood kids play and ride their bikes in the alleyways. There are parks, a library, and specialty stores and cafés line the main street of Monkland Avenue.

Anyone walking the streets of NDG can see the marks of a vibrant community. Before the Christmas holiday season and the first snowfall, houses sport wreaths with hanging red ribbons and magnificent arrays of colored lights. Spring is an awakening period. Season flags on porch columns blow in the wind as planting begins and NDGers head to market for flats of flowers that will spike their front lawns with color.

Being part of a community means that we all contribute our share in an effort to create a hidden bond. There are no rules or regulations as to how a community should function; the only guide is civility. Some argue that signs of civility have to do with cultural attitude, wealth, and tradition: social issues. It's hard, though, to distinguish behavior from the place in which it occurs. People respond favorably to places that instill in them a greater sense of belonging and comfort. Physical attributes that foster a sense of place cannot be orchestrated or artificially introduced—they have to develop by accretion and evolve over time.

One of the challenges that urban planners face with new developments is how to plant the seeds that years later will result in places like Notre-Dame-de-Grâce. What are the visible and hidden elements that make a place pleasant and environmentally comfortable? And why, over the last century, have we witnessed the disappearance of some of these elements from the design of new suburban developments? What needs to be introduced to make them less sterile? In other words, how can we design for civility?

What lends charm to NDG is its density: semi-detached duplexes with their four-family units have meant more residents in each street, more people who decorate their homes and patronize the stores on Monkland Avenue. NDG has what today is considered to be a medium density—twenty-five units per acre (sixty-seven per hectare). The same density and mix of homes and commercial establishments was used by Raymond Unwin and Barry Parker in 1903 in the town of Letchworth, England. Modeling the town after the principles set forth by Ebenezer Howard in his 1902 book *Garden Cities of Tomorrow,* Unwin and Parker suggested a centralized civic area enclosed by a park with housing radiating out all around.

The Garden Suburb, a variant of Howard's concept on the urban edge, turned out to be a more replicable idea in North America. One early instance was Forest Hills Gardens in Queens, New York, designed by the Olmsted brothers and Grosvenor Atterbury in 1911. These years before the war saw great opportunities to transform the planning theory into real towns. A small group of planners, architects, and historians known as the Regional Planning Association became prominent in the planning and execution of these new towns. The RPA lasted from 1923 to 1933 and met two to three times a week, acting as a think tank and a forum for the exchange of ideas. Their goal was to design more humane environments, primarily by acknowledging the Garden City's sensitivities. With "balanced communities, cut to the human scale, in balanced regions" as their credo, they produced some of America's most progressively planned communities and remained influential thinkers and writers in the years that followed.

Radburn, New Jersey, is the most renowned product of the partnership of two of the group's members, Clarence Stein and Henry Wright. After its partial completion in 1929, Radburn became a realistic translation of several of the principles espoused by Howard and earlier put into practice by Unwin and Parker. It served as a model for the form, paradigm, and process of building suburban developments. Though elements were sacrificed in this implementation, the overall result was a safe, healthy community for young families. It had a variety of housing types, and neighborhoods were serviced by small retail centers and defined by cul-de-sacs and scenic, curving streets. Part of Radburn's success was its complete separation of the pedestrian and the automobile. Specialized circulation patterns used interior paths and overpasses, a novel arrangement that inspired a number of new development patterns. As well, the innovative use of the cul-de-sac created "superblocks," each with interior greens spanning 35 to 50 acres (14 to 20 hectares). The dwellings—mostly single-family, along with some rental units in garden apartments—were oriented toward the internal open areas rather than to the streets. Together, these design articulations made Radburn a model of suburban planning for the next fifty years.

Levittown, whose construction began almost twenty years later in 1947, was a different story. This Pennsylvania development looked to Radburn, at least superficially, as a model. Laid out by the Levitt Company on a flat site, the town was designed for a homogeneous population—the young, white, middle-class, car-dependent, Mom-Dad-and-the-kids family. It lacked the Garden City's ideological roots. There was no separation of pedestrian and vehicular traffic and, with little topography with which to respond, the curving streets were arbitrary. Nor was there any localized industry or business—Levittown was intended to house commuters to Philadelphia or to the nearby Fairless Works of United States Steel. The 17,300 houses that were eventually built were spread over 5,750 acres (2,327 hectares) on 1,300 streets—a density of a mere 7 units per acre (17 units per hectare). The town was, in short, a signal exercise in planning inefficiency. The Levittown Company profited handsomely from the development, in whose likeness most of the late twentieth-century's suburbs have been built.

The success of Levittown, coupled with urgent housing demand across the continent, led to the proliferation of low-density developments. Homes were now spread apart and many of the visible amenities of city living were erased. There were no stores, public transit, or small parks—the number of homes on each street didn't justify their existence. Nor were there alleys, which not only provided rear access but were a place where children could play and their parents could meet neighbors and make acquaintances. Land use zoning regulations mandated certain standards for each community, and these standards didn't include alleyway interaction.

The alley space, suburban planners argued, could be replaced by a park area where young and old would have ample room to

THERE GOES THE NEIGHBORHOOD

play or relax. Zoning regulations in most towns stipulated that 10 percent of the total development area would be allocated to this open green space. And while developers found this concentration highly convenient, it did not help to foster community life. Vast parks don't lend themselves to the intimacy of neighbors meeting one another in close quarters. Often these parks were grass-covered open spaces, without even any trees under which to sit. The disappearance of the small park with its play area, trees, and benches, then, meant the loss of a fundamental building block for community.

Another mark of suburbia was its demographic homogeneity. Identical houses were designed for traditional families, with hardly any dwelling diversity within each development. The communities themselves were not made user friendly for the elderly; seniors, developers assumed, would have their own developments with appropriate amenities and facilities. This segregation of North American neighborhoods by household type represented another blow to relationships among citizens. Rather than live close by, children now had to be driven to see their grandparents. Helping an older person cross a busy street or carry grocery bags is an aspect of civil behavior that became a rarity in new developments.

The New Urbanism movement attempted to change the landscape of postwar North American neighborhood planning. Their ideas, introduced in the early 1980s, were modeled after traditional towns. New Urbanists' design schemes reintroduced features that contributed to fostering better relations among residents. As manifested in the town of Seaside, Florida, and later in numerous communities across the continent, New Urbanist designs included pedestrian pockets, smaller setbacks, and town centers with commerce. The movement was a bold realization that older principles can once again foster a sense of civility.

Designing for civility may lie in large-scale issues, some of which have been mentioned above. Many contributing factors, however, have to do with relatively simple small-scale design details—seeds that, when planted, will make a difference years later. It begins at the home itself, by including features that let people personalize and distinguish their residences, and, as a result, the street. Allowing places for planter boxes on windowsills, flag holders on porch columns, and space to plant trees and shrubbery on the front lawn creates opportunities and reminds citizens of the contributions that they can make.

Public benches, for example, absent from new developments, must be made part of the streetscape. They are meeting and resting places to pause and engage in a long conversation. As part of reduced reliance on cars, the use of public transit must be encouraged and bus stops should be placed on street corners. I've met and spoken with many of my neighbors at the stop while waiting for the bus to arrive. In northern cities, bus shelters can be heated and have a seat for the comfort of the elderly.

Creating opportunities for human interaction is what planning for civility is all about. And when these features are put in place at the outset, the chance for a healthy evolution of a neighborhood is set in motion.

# BRING BACK THE SCALE

ON THE FIRST DAY OF A HOUSING DESIGN COURSE THAT I TEACH, I take my students to Coursol Street in Montreal's Little Burgundy neighborhood. Built in the early 1900s to house families with modest incomes, the place has aged well over the years. Standing in the middle of the 25-foot (7.6-meter) wide road with cars parked on each side, I ask my students how the surroundings make them feel. "Comfortable," "domestic," and "safe" are some of the answers I commonly get. Then I ask them what makes them feel that way. The tall trees that form a green canopy over the road, one tells me. No garage doors visible in any of the houses, others notice. The outside stairs, the colorful facades, and the planter boxes that hang from handrails, someone else suggests.

Then we all drive to Dollard-Des-Ormeaux, a forty-year-old neighboring suburban town. There, in the middle of a typical street, I once again ask them about their impressions. The expression on their faces tells it all. As they look around at the wider streets, spread-apart homes, huge garages, manicured lawns fronting spacious, set-back residences with their repetitive facades, they seem disappointed. It's not the same, one answers. When I insist on them finding the single crucial aspect that distinguishes one place from another, they stumble and often leave it out: human scale.

*Scale* refers to the way we proportion our surroundings and relate our own height to the places in which we find ourselves. Suitable urban scale is the outcome of well-proportioned street width, setback of houses from the road, and building height relative to street dimensions. The height of trees and streetlamps also contributes to good scale. When properly designed, parking and vehicular circulation, private and public open spaces, and home and community forms are further ingredients that can instill a sense of urban proportion.

Appropriate scale enhances a sense of comfort with our surroundings. Walking through the streets of Bologna and Sienna—with their particular building height, street width, and storefront proportions—is a pleasant experience. Disproportionate scale, on the other hand, can make us feel out of place and uncomfortable. Standing in the grand hall of the Milan train station, dwarfed by the high ceiling and the imposing statues, is not a pleasant experience.

How was human scale lost in the first place? Are the wide boulevards of North American suburbs necessary when their traffic is so sparse? And why are residents willing to pay so much for their maintenance? Are there urban models with proper human scale in other places that North Americans can learn from and emulate?

The gradual disappearance of human scale can be attributed primarily to reliance on the private motor vehicle and the rise of suburban sprawl. The affordability of the car and the expansion of roads, of course, went hand in hand. The era after the First

World War drew great masses of workers to urban areas across North America. Housing starts in the United States rose by nearly 10 percent annually in the 1920s; by 1930, 48 percent of American households owned their own homes. The car, meanwhile, had become a common fixture in the middle-class lifestyle.

It had initially been considered a glamorous toy for the well-to-do; in 1898, for example, only one automobile was registered per 18,000 Americans. There was neither the infrastructure nor the service facilities to support cars, not to mention the fact that they frequently scared the horses. Then came Henry Ford's affordable and wildly popular Model T. By 1913 the ratio of cars to people had soared to one in eight, and by 1925 Ford's revolutionary factories were producing 9,000 cars per day. When their production stopped in 1927 the United States was home to 26 million cars.

The federal government responded with new policies, technology, and taxes to implement a highway system—highways that quickly became the arteries of American life. Road design made it easy for car and driver, hostile to pedestrians and cyclists. Roads have, in short, grown out of scale.

Parallel to their expanding width was the growing number and quality of the utilities that run alongside or underneath them. As homes began to use more services, more lines were incorporated in street construction. Storm sewer drains, fresh water pipes, electricity, telephone, cable TV, and water for fire hydrants are some of the elements that make up the infrastructure under the pavement. Engineers now play a key role in determining the width of streets and their construction. Fire marshals also started to take part in determining the configuration of roads in neighborhoods. When suburban zoning laws were enacted in the 1950s they were mandated to verify that a 40-foot (12-meter) long fire engine could access every house and turn on every street, ignoring the fact that the fire hydrants are placed every 1,000 feet (300 meters). Designing a shorter truck did not, apparently, enter anyone's mind.

As the number of amenities under the street grew, so did the cost. Paying for infrastructure was at first the responsibility of a municipality through borrowed money. The cost was later transferred to the land developers, who passed them on to residents by including them in the selling price of a new home. The oversized street with its buried amenities now accounts for fully 25 percent of the home's cost, and maintenance, road resurfacing, cleaning, and snow removal have become part of the municipal tax bill. Residents pay huge sums of money for roads they use only once or twice daily. Transportation studies show that suburban streets are used primarily between 7 and 9 a.m. and again between 5 and 7 p.m.—when people are headed to and from work—and sporadically on weekends. The streets are idle the rest of the time.

Municipal bylaws that govern community planning also set houses a minimum of 20 feet (6 meters) and some even 30 feet (9 meters) back from the road, further eroding human scale. One of the principal reasons for the setback was the questionable notion that a wide boulevard made the street look more distinguished. The other reason was access to parking garages, which had become a central preoccupation of car-dependent municipalities, the developers who build them, and the homeowners who buy them.

Pushed up front, garages with their double and often triple doors dominate the built landscape. Sometimes you have to search for the main door or otherwise wonder why houses need to look like a carwash. Making the garage part of a house is a relatively recent phenomenon. The need to store a mode of commuting is not. Parking horse and buggy was part of the human habitat for a long time, and when society organized itself in a permanent, more complex civic form, a common solution had to be found. Be it a mews in London or a carriage house at the back of a mansion in Savannah, parking in its earlier form was born.

The proliferation of the car marked another milestone in the evolution of parking. Cars, smaller in size and fewer in number, replaced the carriage at the rear of the house and were parked in a suitable structure. Since turn-of-the-century, northern-city streets weren't plowed and cars rarely used in the winter, no one had to shovel a snowy driveway. In cities, rear access to open or enclosed parking came by way of alleys, or lanes, which created a secondary transportation network. Alleyways—also the place where kids played, deliveries were made, and trash was collected— disappeared with the birth of suburban land subdivision. Some municipalities regarded them as unsafe. Developers realized that they could add the rear strip of land to each house, making a big backyard even bigger—and suburban homeowners didn't mind having larger yards.

In post–Second World War low-density suburbanization, cars were now used year-round for every household chore. In a busy lifestyle, wasting precious minutes clearing a snowy driveway was unacceptable. The car, then, had to be brought closer to home. In fact, right into it. At first cars were parked underground, in one-car, discreet front or side basement garages. But the number of cars per family soon grew; when a child reached driving age car keys became a "must" gift, Mom and Dad only too eager to relieve themselves of family chauffeur duties. With every member of the family having their own car, coupled with strict bylaws and regulations that in some municipalities mandated up to four parking spots per home, garages had to be located at the front of the house. It was the only place where so many cars, parked in tandem or side by side, could fit. Ironically, garages have become a huge closet for unused household goods. Lawn chairs, lawn mower, bicycles, and suitcases are stored here, while the cars are often parked in the driveway or on the street.

Placing garages up front has also exacted an indirect social toll. Porches had to be left out of front facades, and often not even a window could be placed there. Not only did homeowners lose visual contact with their neighbors, but the wide garage door dominating the front of the house contributed to diminishing scale. Homeowners had less surface to soften and personalize, and since no trees could be planted on a driveway, landscaped gaps between houses created barren streets.

The present state of affairs in suburban planning raises a number of questions. Why should local roads be as wide as Manhattan's

Fifth Avenue? Why should garages dominate the streetscape? We tend to accept that this is how things are, that these practices are forever embodied in zoning bylaws. When one travels abroad, however, it's more common to encounter alternative urban designs with proper human scale. The Dutch, for example, considered the separation between cars and people a long time ago.

It was a chilly spring morning in Meerlo, where I had arrived the previous night to attend a conference. I was up early and left my hotel to walk around this Dutch town on the outskirts of the city of Eindhoven. The townhouse-lined streets were empty. From time to time someone stepped out, offered a greeting, then got into a parked car and drove away. The brick-clad houses had red clay tiled roofs and simple facades. Doorframes were lined up with windows on the upper floors, and most windows had wide, black flower boxes fastened to their sills. Many people had also hung ornaments on the inside of their windows. The streets slowly began to fill with cars and bicyclists, children waving to their parents as they set off to the neighborhood school, well-dressed men and women lining up at the bus stop near an intersection, and older people pausing to speak with one another outside a corner bakery fragrant with the smell of freshly baked bread.

I felt comfortable walking the streets of Meerlo. It was evident that the planners of this small town had proportioned it on a human scale. It appeared that Meerlo had been built after the Second World War. In between the newer homes were recognizably older ones—maybe it had been an old village that expanded over the years. The houses weren't identical, yet there was a definite sense of harmony in the ensemble. They were close to the narrow public sidewalk, set back just 6.5 feet (2 meters) with a narrow strip for meticulously tended gardens. I wondered how such a small strip of land could look so striking. The mature trees' branches reached well over the sidewalks and into the streets. The streetlamps were also well proportioned, and once in a while a street bench was placed alongside one of them. What was most evident in the streets of Meerlo was that people, not cars, owned the road.

Common sense began in the Dutch town with the building of a hierarchy of road widths. Local roads were narrow and did not exceed 25 feet (7.6 meters). There were no front parking garages. Cars were parked in specially designated bays that encroached into the sidewalk parallel to the street, angled or perpendicular to it. Next to the larger houses were covered parking sheds under tall trees. No speed bumps were required, since the narrow street with cars parked on each side prevented motorists from speeding up. Nor were there traffic lights. The intersections were slightly raised and covered with cobblestone, reminding motorists to slow down as they passed through them or turned. Entrances to the streets were narrow, limiting traffic speed. On many of them I noticed kids playing, and they didn't seem threatened or alarmed when a car arrived. The driver would pause for a moment, the road would empty, and the car would pass.

All the streets were lined with bicycle paths. I looked at the bikes as they passed by: these were not leisure riders. Most of the bikes had baskets with groceries or schoolbags affixed to their front or rear—Meerlo's citizens obviously relied on their bikes as much as or even more than their cars for local trips. The bicycle paths were paved differently than the roads themselves, clearly distinguishing the two traffic realms.

Near the neighborhood center of Meerlo the streetscape changed once more. The sidewalk disappeared and blended in with the road itself. Known in Holland as *Woonorf*, this kind of street was designed to be shared by pedestrians and motorists. The distinct street surface made walking comfortable and safe, and the tall trees on edges created the feel of a public square or even a park.

Meerlo is not unique; similar urban settings are spread across Europe. The cultural, historic, and climatic conditions of these towns are, of course, different, yet the very same common sense can and already does (to a lesser degree) prevail in North America. Concerns about the effect of urban sprawl and a call for the increased density of new communities offer a chance to bring human scale back to neighborhoods. It is imperative, however, that several steps be taken to ensure that densification not become another missed opportunity in the design of new developments. Public transit must be made efficient and affordable and planned so that it can reach as many streets as possible. Not all public transport will be profitable, but it can be made cost-effective. The private motor vehicle should not be the only mode of commuting.

Attention should also be given to road design itself. A local street width of 25 feet (7.6 meters) is quite appropriate for both private and public motor vehicles. Many narrow Parisian streets, for example, have cars parked on both sides with space for a traffic lane still left down the middle. It makes even greater sense when you consider the popularity of compact economy cars. And although northern towns have to cope with snow, one parking lane should be sufficient here, since most homeowners have garages. Municipalities concerned with the burden of snow removal will simply have to pass that burden on to the home-owners themselves, who in return will live on a nice street.

Let's also consider the merit of recessing garages. The homes themselves could be placed closer to the curb in order to make more space for a garage at the rear, either next to the building or accessed via a lane. Then there's the idea of shared parking. Townhouses, for example, could have a common underground parking garage tucked in the rear, with backyards built on top.

Having a parking structure is another idea worth pursuing. Every group of homes could have a structure located a short walking distance away—well integrated into the home's design and land-scaped to make it less noticeable. The less expensive alternative is aboveground common parking with small numbers of cars and plug-in receptacles for cold winter nights. As in European neigh-borhoods, they can be nicely integrated with trees to provide shade in summertime. Finally, there's street parking to consider, an option that some municipalities have banned in the name of snow removal and fire truck passage. It's time to revisit the merit of these decrees.

Narrowing streets and relocating garages can be a first important step in bringing back human scale to new neighborhoods. We can also advocate building taller rather than wider homes. The long-forgotten attic can be reintroduced: changing the roof angle and introducing a dormer will lend more appeal to the home and the street. Suitable trees should also be mandatory. In many new communities very young trees or shrubs are planted, and these take years to reach a height ample enough to create proper scale. Encouraging people to plant additional trees and care for the old ones can also help.

Homeowners tend to believe that their domain ends at the edge of their lot and that the street belongs to someone else—the city perhaps. Residents ought to recognize that the street in front of their home is theirs as well. As in many North American neighborhoods, roads can be designed with narrow edges at each end. This makes them easy to close, turning the street into a neighborhood public square where residents could hold a community-wide barbecue or a giant yard sale. Similar to some European towns, a mobile food market can set up shop on the street on weekends, reducing the need to travel to the big box at the edge of town.

As we plan our future neighborhoods and fix existing ones, we may want to take a hard look at our streets and reclaim them. After all, it is we who pay for their costly construction and never-ending upkeep. Doing so will also help foster a sense of safety and bring neighborhoods together as stronger communities.

# REINVENTING CITIES

CHUCK CHARLEBOIS GREETED ME AS I STEPPED OFF THE TRAIN IN Cornwall, Ontario. After we made each other's acquaintance, he suggested that we head to his car. Charlebois had invited me to Cornwall to help a local nonprofit group prepare a plan for the rehabilitation of Le Village, one of the town's districts, and for the conversion of several empty industrial buildings to affordable housing.

It was a crisp, sunny winter day. The streets and sidewalks of the Eastern Ontario town of 50,000 on the shores of the St. Lawrence Seaway were covered with snow. Charlebois, the spokesperson for Renaissance, the nonprofit group, pointed to one of the homes. "I was born in this one, and have lived all my life in Le Village," he said. The neglect in the poverty-stricken district was apparent. Some of the wooden porches were decaying and a few houses badly needed a fresh coat of paint. The windows and doors of others were boarded up with plywood.

"Times were better when I was growing up here," Charlebois recalled. "It was a thriving community. People had jobs and pride. We cared about each other and about Le Village." We turned onto Montreal Road and drove by a gray stone church with a tall steeple. "This is the Church of the Nativity," he pointed out. "It's still the heart of our mostly French-Canadian community. Only a few worshippers pray here these days. Many have moved away."

We pulled into a parking lot. A huge five-story brown brick industrial building with boarded windows stood ahead of us. A block-long, three-story structure was behind us, parallel to the nearby shoreline. Two more structures were farther away. It was quiet, and no passersby were about. We stood there surveying the area until Charlebois suggested that we step in. He unlocked a metal door and turned on the lights. Several rows of fluorescent fixtures lit up the vast space, permeated by a strong smell of industrial oil. Weaving machinery lay idle in one of the corners along with piles of big bundles of cotton. It looked as if the life had been suddenly switched off.

We climbed one floor up, where the scene was much the same. A thick layer of dust covered the thick, oily floor planks. Flocks of pigeons flew from one end of the hall to another, nearly hitting the columns. "I got my first job here," Charlebois said. "I was a clerk. Most of my relatives, friends, and neighbors worked here at one time." He removed a sheet of plywood from one of the windows; the St. Lawrence Seaway stretched out in the distance. We stood there quietly, looking at the abandoned industrial buildings nearby and the sparkling water in the distance.

"What do you think?" Charlebois asked me as we stepped out into the sunny day. I looked back at the tall, imposing structure and told him that I believed in these buildings' potential. I knew, however, that a lot of work lay ahead.

As we drove back to the train station I thought about the rise and decline of the city of Cornwall. I wondered if the current situation could have been predicted back then and prepared for. Could anyone have foreseen that the textile industry would decline one day? Should our cities' destinies be regarded as simply an act of god or is there some rationale in our faith in urban systems? How can you guarantee that other North American neighborhoods won't experience the fate of Le Village? The evolution of cities provides some revealing insight into many of these questions.

Until the Industrial Revolution, North America was largely rural. In 1820 cities were home to only 7 percent of the American population (a similar ratio prevailed in Canada), the majority of whom lived in either New York or Philadelphia. Only ten cities in the United States could boast populations greater than 10,000. This didn't last long: as the Industrial Revolution spread from England to North America, urban populations skyrocketed. By 1860 New York City had over one million residents, and seven other cities exceeded 100,000. By 1890 New York City was approaching the size of London, with a million living in Philadelphia and Chicago, respectively. Half of all the people in the northeastern United States had become urban, as had one-third of America's entire population.

Pre-industrial cities had high densities and clearly defined city limits. Mixed land use gave people the luxury of living close to their workplace; often, the most respectable addresses were at the city's core. But when industries moved into the core to access cheap immigrant labor and transportation hubs, the noise, dirt, and density thus generated greatly impaired urban livability. Exodus from the city was an option only for the rich.

Industrial production relied on power sources, which gave rise to towns like Cornwall that were located along waterways. Canals and rivers were also instrumental as a means of moving raw materials and finished goods to and from industries. But when electricity began to power machinery and railroads became widespread, the fortune of some cities started to decline. Later developments led to further decline: after the Second World War, new industries and highly efficient production methods emerged that would eclipse older industries and render the multi-floor factory obsolete. Moving goods in and out of crowded cities came to be regarded as slow and inefficient, and high city taxes added to the burden.

Manufacturing facilities abandoned their old methods of production and moved to the periphery of towns. And as trucks gained prominence over ships and trains, locating a plant next to a highway became essential. When industries left the city, so did people: urban overpopulation made suburbia a choice place to live. It was a highly convenient arrangement for all except the cities, where old neighborhoods were left behind and once-vibrant industrial buildings become vacant.

Tougher foreign competition also affected industrial production. As low-wage labor markets in the developing world began to

THERE GOES THE NEIGHBORHOOD

welcome offshore industries, labor-intensive production in North America declined rapidly. Remnants of the old economy were replaced by the new. The rise of the service industry coincided with the proliferation of computers that were designed here but manufactured overseas for much lower costs. Those cities that weathered the transition, however, began to see their fortunes rise again.

Many North American cities encouraged people to move back by offering monetary incentives. Others attempted to cope with years of neglect, decay, and blight. Some municipal administrators realized that, since roads and infrastructure already existed, revitalizing their city could be cost effective. They had to make the city a livable place, though, and some, like Minneapolis, built hockey arenas and ballparks in the downtown core; others opened markets and malls in abandoned buildings. And so it was that, during the 1990s, older cities like Seattle and Chicago were revived. Living downtown in new or converted industrial buildings next to cultural and shopping amenities became fashionable, and followed the emergence of nontraditional households. Singles, young couples without children, and the elderly all made city living their choice.

But the question remains: how should cities prepare for their future? If the history of industrial development is any indication, boom and bust cycles will continue to affect the well-being of cities. What's needed is a flexible decision-making and design process that will let municipal leaders alter previous plans.

Some cities weren't quick enough to change land uses, believing that another new industry would take the place of an old one. Others were able to save districts by switching rapidly from commercial to residential, permitting conversion of old factories to loft apartments.

Attempts to rejuvenate cities by building shopping centers and stadiums were risky endeavors. It was assumed that these establishments would draw people from suburbs to town—and they have, but only for a short period each week. In order to succeed, cities need to create an environment that never sleeps, to attract establishments that stay open after sunset and draw the kind of people who patronize them. The percentage of nontraditional families is expected to rise, and they'd rather have museums, theaters, and cafés than backyard swimming pools and barbecues.

City homes themselves should be allowed to adapt according to demographic and economic trends. Dividing a single residence into separate households, or creating a home office on the ground floor or in a rear ancillary structure, can be accomplished without compromising the residential character of a neighborhood. People should further be allowed to add floors or convert empty attics to rental units. If a decline begins, only by introducing such preparatory measures will urban districts stand a chance of riding out changes to emerge healthy again.

Cornwall's past is no different from that of many other North American cities. Industrial development began here when the

Cornwall Canal was completed in 1843 and generated the necessary energy to turn a small agricultural settlement into an industrial powerhouse. Local government granted water power privileges to cotton mill operations soon thereafter, and over the next twenty years sawmill factories sprang up on the land east of the canal.

In order to limit competition in the cotton industry, in 1892 all the mills were merged into the Canadian Coloured Cotton Mills Company. Most of its early employees were of Scottish descent, but by the late 1880s about half were French-speaking, and it was they who named the neighborhood Le Village. Numerous businesses started up to service the mill workers and their families. The vast majority of the houses in Le Village were built between 1880 and 1950 to house them, roughly correlating with the active years of the cotton mills, with a temporary halt in construction during the war.

Cornwall started to go down in 1959 when the Seaway was completed and the power-generating canal was rendered obsolete. A more efficient way of producing textiles was also introduced, obviating the need to haul bundles of cotton and finished goods from floor to floor. Foreign competition was another blow to the textile industry. Countries with lower wages scooped up jobs, leaving employment scars in the city. When the Canada Cotton Mill ceased operations in the late 1950s, 1,700 jobs were lost and 3,260 citizens became welfare recipients. In the 1960s and 1970s, with so many people moving out to find employment elsewhere, owner-occupied homes were bought up by a few speculators who converted them into rental properties. Since the housing stock was, and still is, fairly old and not improved upon, and since a high vacancy rate made for cheaper rents than the rest of Cornwall, Le Village attracted people from the lower-income brackets. The traditional ills of poorer communities began to dilute the once strong sense of community pride and unity.

I called Charlebois the next day and told him that I'd be willing to act as consultant for his group. Over the following four years, assisted by students, I began to tackle some of the city's challenges. First, we recognized that it needed a makeover of sorts to shake its industrial image. It would also have to take advantage of its greatest asset, the location along the river, and find a new use for the empty cotton mill building. A variety of ideas poured forth: a streetcar that ran on Main Street half a century ago could be brought back to life, for example, and an abandoned industrial area near the waterfront could be transformed into a residential community. At one point we discovered that a small power station turbine in one of the buildings had been designed by Edison himself. Why not rehabilitate it and build a textile museum on the ground level? The spacious upper floors had plenty of room for light wells—covered atriums—in their centers. The municipality could build interior gardens, balconies, jogging tracks, and a swimming pool overlooking the river.

The rehabilitation of Le Village itself came next. Some of the decaying homes could be replaced by new ones and others renovated. A program, we suggested, should be established to assist homeowners financially in upgrading their facades and converting their homes to other uses they might want, as long as it was in keeping with the local architectural character.

The wheels started to turn again in Cornwall. But the economic ups and downs this city has experienced will likely bring about similar challenges to other cities. What concerned leaders need to do is keep a watchful eye out and retain a flexible plan. City dwellers can do their part by patronizing local establishments, just one of many ways they can help create a vibrant urban environment.

# HOUSING THE TREES

WHEN JEAN-MARIE LAVOIE AND PAUL BRASSARD INVITED ME TO collaborate with them, I couldn't help but be a little skeptical. The pair, retired architects, had recently bought a 100-acre (40-hectare) wood in St. Nicolas, a little town near Quebec City. What they wanted was to build a community there where trees would be as important as houses.

On a sunny fall day I drove out to meet them. Lavoie had given me directions to his house, which was perched at the top of a ravine at the edge of the forest. A gushing stream below flowed into the St. Lawrence River. Lavoie, a tall, bearded man who speaks French with a northern Quebec accent, spotted me through his front window and stepped out to greet me. After he retired from running a busy architectural firm with his partner Brassard, he told me, he built the house himself. "I woke up one day and asked myself what I wanted to do for the rest of my life, and decided that I needed a change," he recalled. "We designed museums, schools, and hospitals and won awards and recognitions, but both Paul and I decided that it was time to quit."

Lavoie suggested we go inside. Amélie Chiasson, his wife, greeted me in a soft voice. The interior was modestly decorated, with large windows on the south side that let in plenty of sun. The doorbell rang and Brassard walked in. The silver-haired partner introduced himself and joined us around the table as Amélie served coffee. In the distance, through the northern window, I could see a boat on the St. Lawrence.

"Why would you undertake the building of a development now that you've retired?" I asked them. "Since my retirement, I've often walked in the forest," Lavoie told me. "I know every trail, path, and tree. I fell in love with the scenery. Then I heard that the property was rezoned for housing development. I know what a developer will do to the forest if a conventional approach is followed. One day I saw a For Sale sign. I called Paul, consulted with Amélie, and we all decided to buy the forest and try to do something different." "Why not just leave it as it is?" I asked. "We considered that too," Brassard responded. "But we realized that we'd all be better served by turning it into a kind of demon-stration project, showing that clearing trees and boulders isn't a required step in home building."

Lavoie suggested that we walk in the forest. The sun was begin-ning to set and a light breeze was blowing. As we made our way on a narrow path, he pointed to a footprint of a deer. He and his partner identified species of trees and their ages and named shrubs. When we arrived at a ravine with boulders jutting out they pointed to a rock formation and explained the effect that tree roots have on the soil. We continued to walk quietly, bypassing fallen tree trunks and climbing over big rocks. Soon a wide vista opened up at the edge of a huge cliff. The St. Lawrence River spread out below us and Quebec City buildings started to light up in the distance as we stood there, silently admiring the view. On our walk back I asked for some time to reflect on their offer.

Achieving what Lavoie and Brassard wanted wouldn't be easy. Over the years I've worked with numerous developers who would often shrug off environmental concerns. And developers aren't the only ones at fault. Current municipal bylaws, the rules that govern residential development standards, make it hard to conserve the site's natural resources and beauty, including its trees. The insistence on wide roads and lots is a strike against any attempt to break with a conventional approach. I feared that, despite our best intentions, we would fail. Yet I was intrigued by the prospect of designing a different community. I wondered what kind of neighborhoods could have been created in North America if municipal authorities and their developers had been more creative and flexible in their decision making. If we had been given the opportunity to start from a clean slate, what would have been done differently? And is preserving natural resources today at all realistic given current development practices and pressures?

The need to find a middle ground between preservation and development began to be debated in the mid-1970s. What triggered the debate was the harm development practices had done to the environment. In his 1973 landmark book *Small Is*

*Beautiful: Economics as if People Mattered,* E.F. Schumacher warned of actions that, if pursued further, could endanger the delicate balance between people and nature. Years later his warnings helped galvanize an international attempt to outline specific actions to remedy the situation. The World Commission on Environment and Development, also known as the Brundtland Commission, is probably the best-known international initiative. In their 1987 report *Our Common Future,* the commissioners defined sustainable development as that which "meets the present without compromising the ability of future generations to meet their own needs." A conceptual approach whereby every present action has to be taken while considering its future effect on the environment was put in place.

The report cited three main factors that influence the functioning of a sustainable community. The first is society itself: the demographic makeup and lifestyles of the people who live in the development. The second is the development's economic vitality. Third is the environment itself, whose many facets include both natural and built features. Only when a balance is struck between these three elements in a way that takes the future into consideration is sustainable development possible.

Since the turn of the twentieth century, and particularly since the Second World War, bad development practices have taken their toll. Agricultural land and forested landscape alike were cleared to make room for wide roads and houses. Vast, green natural spaces were covered with sod that required gallons of fresh water during dry summer months. North Americans consumed domestic space much like any other product, and houses swelled in size. And as home design became more intricate and complex, ever more trees were felled for their construction. Keeping houses warm in winter and cool in summer, consuming fresh water, draining gray water, and creating domestic waste all inflict short- and long-term damage to both local and global environments.

It was clear that old practices needed to be abandoned and new ones put in place. Sustainable residential development set out to reduce reliance on cars by encouraging public transit, pedestrian travel, and the mix of commercial and residential uses. Alternative building products and practices that consume fewer natural resources became widespread. Attention was paid to constructing better-insulated homes that consume less energy, and designers oriented houses to maximize solar gain.

I called Lavoie the next day and told him I'd be interested in collaborating with him and Brassard. The more I reflected on the design challenge, the more fascinated I became. The logical course of action, I thought, would be to leave the site untouched—but there had to be a way to strike a realistic balance between nature and development. Those who advocate sustainable development don't intend to bring residential construction to a screeching halt, but rather to reform development practices so that we can, as it were, see the forest for the trees.

We recognized from the beginning that proper decisions would need to be made each step of the way, from site planning to house design. Conservation of resources must be made equal to all other priorities. We needed to design homes that would be affordable, that would correspond to the needs of an evolving demographic, and that would consume the least resources before and after occupancy.

We began by taking stock of the site's natural conditions, carefully marking on a map its boulder formations, ravines, and hilly areas. Some areas had very young trees and shrubs, while others had concentrations of old growth. When we agreed that our knowledge wasn't sufficient to assess the status of a tree, a forestry expert was called in. The natural state of the site started to emerge.

After the site was audited we began looking for appropriate road paths. Here, too, we broke with tradition. Without specific zoning for this virgin site we could come up with our own master plans and sets of guidelines. Conventional 40-foot (12-meter) wide roads wouldn't make sense in our case, nor would the building of a 5-foot (1.5-meter) sidewalk. In our search for alternatives we visited the neighboring village of St. Nicolas. Its streets were 20 feet (6 meters) wide, which not only saved precious land but lent the old village a pleasing human scale. We agreed that this width would also serve us well. The sidewalks in a low-density community like ours should also be appropriately designed, and we eventually decided on an 18-inch (0.4-meter) wide concrete path laid level with the street itself, letting rainwater return to where it belongs—nature.

Subdividing the land into plots of equal shape and size wouldn't make sense; whereas suburban communities developed under similar conditions often feature one-size-fits-all lots (60 by 100 feet/18 by 30 meters), what we wanted were lot dimensions that would vary according to topography and housing density. The long, narrow lot, we agreed, would be best because it would avoid sprawling houses and help preserve trees. No cutting of trees outside the houses' footprint would be allowed.

Houses would be brought closer to the road, and instead of garages we'd create parking structures. The dense area in the middle and at the top of the site, we decided, would be turned into a communal park. Burying telephone, cable TV, and electricity wires under the road also helped leave the site in its natural condition.

Our quest to limit the number of trees cut led us on a search for a housing form that suited the site conditions. Rather than building wide, we decided to build narrow and tall. We chose a design with a 20-by-32 foot (6-by-10 meter) floor dimension. This created 650-square-foot (59-square-meter) floors, each of which could become a self-contained one-bedroom apartment.

During construction we took special precautions to protect the trees, wrapping them to guard against damage caused by heavy machinery. Recognizing the effect that extensive excavation and dynamiting would have on the environment, we also decided to avoid a basement level and to build a shallow foundation instead. We took advantage of the attic with a special truss design that allowed maximal use of the space under the roof. Turning the attic into a habitable area would also help conserve energy: since warm air rises, there would be less need to heat the space during the winter months.

When we began thinking about house design we realized that we had to first conceive the makeup of the entire community. The identical sizes and prices of houses in traditional developments attract homeowners with similar economic and social characteristics, whereas we envisioned a neighborhood with people of mixed ages and lifestyles. In order to amplify choice and adaptability we had to come up with an appropriate floor plan. This meant locating all the wet functions and services along one of the walls, freeing the rest of the space for interior partitioning that would fit the occupants' needs and budgets. The stairs, kitchen, bathrooms, and utilities were all placed against the north wall, which led to further advantages: the windowless wall reduced energy loss and made for greater privacy from the neighboring house. Windows on the southern elevation increased exposure and maximized solar gain.

This open-ended design approach allowed us to create a variety of interior configurations. The ground floor could be an independent dwelling to house an elderly member of the extended family, for example, or it could become a home office for those who lived on the upper two floors. We also designed two front doors so that the structure could function as either a single- or multi-family home. As well, the configuration of the stairs would permit the installation of an internal elevator to let a disabled person reach all the levels.

Communities are created by accretion; it takes many decades for a place to mature. A mark of a good community is how well it fits in with its surroundings and how little it reshapes what was there before. It is the responsibility of designers and builders to ensure as little disruption as possible. If we're set on preserving resources for future generations, we ought to begin by examining current development practices and changing them for the better. Our St. Nicolas development was a modest step in this direction.

As time went on, homes began to fill the void between the trees in the forest of St. Nicolas. Lavoie and Brassard continued to preach the gospel of tree preservation to the many visitors who came to be inspired by their accomplishment. Some of these visitors took the message home with them to their own communities—demonstrating that citizens have the power to guard their surroundings.

# NUTS AND JOISTS

# THEY DON'T BUILD THEM LIKE THEY USED TO

GLEN STOOD IN A CLOUD OF DUST, CHISELING TILES OFF MY bathroom wall. He sweated as he paused from time to time, grabbing pieces off the floor and throwing them into the half-full wheelbarrow that stood in the hallway nearby. Occasionally he'd use an oversized hammer to knock out a resistant tile. Suddenly the hammering stopped. "Look at that," Glen said, wiping the dust off an area he'd just uncovered. An intricate checkered pattern of 4-by-4 inch (10-by-10 centimeter) black and white glazed ceramic tiles had revealed itself. Glen examined them as if he'd just made an important archaeological discovery. One of the house's previous owners, it seemed, had laid the tiles on top of an older, probably original layer. "Look how they're placed next to each other. There's hardly any grout in between. And look at how the end tile's edges curve." He gestured to the meeting point between the tiles and the door's molding, explaining that the carpenter who made the moldings likely fitted his design to the tile's edge. Glen turned to me. "They don't build them like they used to," he noted regretfully.

Several years after moving into our house my wife and I decided to renovate the bathroom. We hated the awkwardly laid yellowish brown tiles, the mustard-colored fixtures, and the standard, ready-to-install dark brown cabinet. The entry door was a plain hollowcore Luan. The uninsulated floor was cold in winter and an electric baseboard had replaced the cast-iron radiators of the other rooms. The bathroom, in short, stood in marked contrast to the rest of the house.

We'd bought the old home because we liked the neighborhood and we could afford it. But there was something else that made us like the place: the distinctively old atmosphere embedded in the house itself. We appreciated the craftsmanship expressed in its interior details and felt that these simple ornaments made it an *objet d'art*. There were many not-so-hidden signs that turned the house into a home.

The metal flowerbox just outside the front windows is a charming piece of ornamental iron. The transom above the entry door is made of small squares of stained glass, and the sun shining through them lets a special quality of light into the foyer that forms brown squares on the natural-stone floor tiles. Elsewhere, the floor is made of identical strips of maple the shade of honey. Curved and square vaulted arches separate rooms and passageways, and the door frames are engraved with bevelled and right-angle corners.

The house, identical to others on the street, was built in the 1930s for middle-class families. There was a sense of pride and careful attention to detail on the part of the tradesmen who

NUTS AND JOISTS

crafted them. Despite similar proportions, each house has notable details that distinguish one from the next, yet the ensemble creates a nice harmony. The brick pattern and the top edge of the front facade are unique in every one. Old front doors are made of oak and each has its own glass arrangement. When lights shine inside at night you can spot the myriad stained-glass design details; it feels as though you're walking through a huge art gallery.

They certainly don't build them like this anymore. A visit to a new tract-housing development reveals the plainness of today's interiors. Gone are the days of attention to detail. Mass production reigns. You rarely see a plaster molding on the ceiling edge of a living or dining room or a medallion in the room's center from which a chandelier is hung. The floor, if it's made of wood strips, is plain with no borders or intricate patterns. New on-site carpentry and custom-designed details hardly exist. And the investments that are made in finishes are often limited to luxury comfort items. Homeowners, it seems, would rather spend on a whirlpool bath with a built-in TV than on crafted metal or detailed woodworking. Some might not even be aware of the architectural features available, but they'd surely appreciate them years later when the house ages gracefully.

When I visit tract housing, I wonder why the builders or designers stopped including such details in their blueprints. And why do homebuyers no longer demand them? What does this reveal about society's value system? Have we turned our back on the arts or forgotten to include architecture among them? Why do some who yearn for the well-crafted old details of North American homes or pay handsomely for antique furniture decide to exclude them from the construction of their own new house?

For centuries, home building was the domain of master builders. A group of tradespeople, headed by a master who was contracted to construct an edifice, formed a team. Although they'd all be engaged in most phases of building, one member would be more able in framing, for example, while another would handle the masonry work. The design and architecture profession did not exist. Clients relied on the master's skills and knowledge, which were passed on to him by an earlier generation of builders. The master listened to his client's wishes and converted them to plans. Few drawings existed; the intricate details rested in the builder's mind. Design styles lasted for centuries, with craftspersons evolving and perfecting the details over years.

Builders' work was of varying degrees of quality. There were those who constructed homes for the masses, buying a plot of land, constructing a dwelling, selling it, and proceeding on to the next. These were the forefathers of present-day developers. And then there were those who mastered their craft to construct homes for the well-to-do. They would command higher pay, spend more time—sometimes years at a building site—and often move from town to town, where they were invited as their reputations spread.

European building traditions migrated to North America along with their skilled craftsmen. Details had to be modified to meet new weather conditions and local raw materials. Since manufacturing processes were rudimentary, most building components were built on site. A stonemason or finish carpenters were contracted to do specialty work. Carpenters would arrive during construction and consult with the owner or the master builder as to the type of moldings, doors, or flooring design they were planning to use. They would open a pattern book showing woodworking details they were accustomed to producing, later returning to their shop to fabricate these items and then coming back to install them. In large towns, workshops were located next to waterways that powered their wood-sawing or drilling machines. Tools were often invented by the craftsmen themselves when the task or design required it.

This industry began to transform at the turn of the century when the Industrial Revolution and massive migration to cities created the need for an efficient way to build. The master builder and his team of tradespeople building one dwelling at a time gave way to a new paradigm: a single person initiating and overseeing the process and assigning the different tasks to specialized trades. The process, in other words, became decentralized. A bricklayer owned a bricklaying firm and a carpenter a carpentry finishing company; they each specialized in a single task.

The quest for greater efficiency didn't leave much time for intricate construction details. Building components that slowed the process, like elaborate brickwork on a facade, had to be abandoned in favor of plainer ones. No longer was time needed for a craftsperson to visit a building site for measurements, return to his shop for fabrication, and head back to the site for fitting. The tradespeople themselves, with their tools and skills that had evolved over centuries, began to disappear as old-fashioned traditions were replaced by factory-produced products.

The post–Second World War era saw the building industry employ mass production to a greater extent. The large-scale developments that were built to meet the overwhelming housing demand required new efficiencies. One solution was prefabrication; by 1951 one-fifth of an average house was made of components that were prefabricated in a plant. Mass-produced housing meant compact, efficient design, economical construction techniques, and persuasive marketing strategies. The popularity of these houses also led to the creation of nearly instant communities, and, of course, to the virtual elimination of the skilled tradesperson and the architect from the building process.

Along with the birth of the modern homebuilding industry, the trades themselves got organized and unionized. They now commanded higher pay, meaning that labor accounted for a higher share of overall cost. Lowering these labor costs required a builder to minimize on-site time. Complex building components were moved from the building site to a factory floor where sophisticated machinery could produce them for less. Window manufacturing, for example, became an entirely mechanized process, as did the production of cabinetry and vinyl and aluminum siding.

Meanwhile, the rising cost of specialty woods as a result of overharvesting, as well as transport expenses, virtually eliminated their use. Beautiful wood species like African mahogany or Californian cherry that not long ago could have been spotted in middle-class homes and furnishings became prohibitively expensive. Molding, flooring, doors, and built-ins were produced from cheaper materials and were often painted over.

Along with the disappearance of the building details themselves, public regard of a home as an *objet d'art* declined. When asked why they aren't investing in fine details, builders claim that not many buyers are willing to pay for them. Society has changed, and so have attitudes toward craftsmanship. With rampant consumerism and frequent mobility, homes have become a traded commodity. For some they're a short-term investment portfolio item, not a place where generations will live but a shelter with appreciating value. And a house with a large bathroom equipped with a whirlpool bath and multi-jet shower often yields a higher resale value than one with an intricate woodwork pattern on the floor.

The question remains as to whether these details are forever gone. Some wonder if societal attitudes will shift again and good workmanship in homes will reappear. But if that happens, how will we be able to trace long-gone knowledge and extinct materials? Two phenomena suggest cause for hope: technological innovation in materials and production and the rising interest in remodeling. Visit any renovation center and you'll readily see manifestations of both.

You can park two jumbo jets side by side in some big-box renovation stores. A Saturday visit to a Home Depot shows how popular these centers have become. The Atlanta-based company was founded in 1978 and, at the end of 2003, was operating 1,707 stores in 47 states, as well as in most Canadian provinces, Puerto Rico, Chile, and Argentina. Crowds of do-it-yourselfers stroll through aisles that are loaded with paint cans, shower stalls, and plywood sheets. North Americans are renovating, and renovation has become a big business. Over the past decade Canadians have invested a whopping $20 billion in renovation, an amount that exceeds that of new construction. According to an Industry Canada report, in the past two years homeowners and renters have spent an average of $4,313 and $1,856, respectively, on their renovation projects. A closer examination of the products themselves reveals that change has occurred there, too.

Some items that have reappeared are old-fashioned ceiling rosettes (the molded circle in the middle of the ceiling), nicely shaped floor and door moldings, wonderfully curved ceiling edges, Art Deco–like light fixtures, Queen Anne–style door handles, and bathtubs with brass legs. Products like these have returned because manufacturers have recognized trends in the marketplace and hope to tap in to this potential. They also have new technologies and composite materials at their disposal. Computers can now trace and build the molds of old forms, replacing the steady hands of old artisans with sophisticated, programmable machines that can produce low-cost items with extreme accuracy and speed.

Along with the new machines came new raw materials. Lumber is no longer brought from the Amazonian rain forest, but there's no shortage of medium-density fiberboard, extruded plastics, and soft recycled metals. Cast gypsum and molded synthetic wood products help create ceiling edges and kitchen cabinet doors. It's ironic that, at the dawn of a new century, cutting-edge technology is used to recreate old artifacts and traditions. Some say we're faking it. But innovation has always been an evolutionary process, and it ought to be no different in the realm of building products. We've replaced the craftsperson with a machine, but we've kept the craft.

Along with a change in materials, processing, and product manufacturing, we've witnessed a resurgence of interest in home renovation itself. People have gotten more comfortable with using tools. Many have well-stocked cabinets with power drills and other sophisticated machinery. Complete sets of wrenches and screwdrivers are also common. Neatly stored in their garages are folded workbenches, and often the garage itself has a mini-workshop. This phenomenon can be attributed in part to the proliferation of television shows, magazines, and newspaper articles that have made home renovation all the more enticing. These shows demonstrate the mechanics of renovation work in a simple, accessible way. Some of the projects explained on these shows seem overly complex, yet the TV producers have achieved something remarkable: the transformation of remodeling into entertainment. More important, they've raised public interest in preserving the old.

Perhaps the greatest step forward in home renovation is the evolution of the tools themselves. Manufacturers have reoriented their products toward the most popular market segment: the homeowners. They have, in other words, redesigned and packaged them to be used by everyone. Here, too, new materials have contributed a great deal. Plastic pipes, for example, have eclipsed cast-iron and copper plumbing. The soldering of metal pipes has been replaced by dry connections, simplifying installation for the layperson. Smart designs have increased products' longevity, and clear instructions have made them easier to install. Many now contain fewer components that require assembly. New faucets, for example, are designed with a single lever that reduces the number of moving parts and facilitates their use. Opening a package and trying to figure out where each piece belongs has become, for the most part, a thing of the past.

NUTS AND JOISTS

Further evolution in the design of products is inevitable, and a new generation of advanced metals and plastics will make them last even longer. And just take a look at the latest models: a door handle or a light fixture or a faucet, you'll notice, is a potential masterpiece.

# WEATHERING THE STORM

ON JANUARY 5, 1998, MY CITY CAME TO A STANDSTILL THAT would last for two weeks. Two days earlier I had returned from a vacation abroad. I was in the midst of a sabbatical leave and looked forward to devoting the next little while to writing.

It all started with steady downpour of ice pellets which later that morning turned into rain. Then the temperature dipped, and the freezing rain started coating everything with ice. This happens in Montreal occasionally; when a warm, moving air mass glides over a stationary cold one, the layering results in the formation of freezing rain and ice pellets. In January 1998, though, *three* successive masses of warm, moist air traveled northward from the Gulf of Mexico. Warm and cold air met above the Saint Lawrence Valley and remained there longer than usual: five whole days.

The rain hadn't stopped by the end of that first day. The tree branches in front of our house began to bend under the weight of the ice, and ice-coated cars parked along the sidewalk looked as if a magic spell had gone horribly wrong. Down the street, a man chiseled his way with an ice scraper and cleared the lock of his vehicle's door. The thick electric cables that stretched from the hydro poles across the street onto the roof of each house were unusually low above the road as the ice on them continued to mount. I wondered how long they'd withstand the burden.

It got a bit colder as the hours went by, but we were all comfortable at home. TV weather reports forecast freezing rain throughout the night. I went around the house making sure that all the windows were firmly shut, and raised the thermostat up high in case it got colder. Soon the humming of the furnace in the basement got louder. Our natural gas furnace circulates hot water through pipes that feed the cast-iron radiators underneath each window on our floor and in the apartment above. There are no radiators in the basement, only a few electrical baseboards that we installed when we renovated the space.

I woke up to an eerie silence. The numbers on my bedside digital clock were off. It was pitch black. I reached for my wristwatch in the bedside drawer and saw that it was 4:10 a.m. My wife was asleep, and when I went down the hallway to our kids' bedrooms I saw them curled up under blankets. No longer was a humming sound coming from the basement. Along with the power failure, the water circulation pump had stopped.

The streetlights and the lights in the houses were all off. Still, I could see the area out front: it looked like a war zone with all the tree branches lying across it. Farther away, a branch had fallen atop a parked car, causing considerable damage. An electric power cable lay on the ground, one end connected to the wooden pole and the other to the fittings that connect the cables to my neighbor's house. Given the weight of the ice and all the fallen tree branches, more power lines were likely torn down in the neighborhood and beyond. It looked like we'd be out of power for a while.

Hoping to keep the heat in, I rolled up a couple of blankets and put them against the bottom of the front and back doors. When my wife woke up I told her what had happened. A new term was beginning at her university that day and she needed to get there to teach an early class. Since elementary school classes were to begin a few days later, the kids would stay at home with me.

The day broke and our children woke up. The street looked even grimmer in daylight, the large fallen branches blocking traffic. As the temperature began to drop in the house I lit a fire in the living room fireplace and we congregated in front of it. On a battery-operated radio I heard a news report about the extent of the damage in the entire province and the forecast for continuing freezing rain. The entire grid was damaged. How long would the house stay warm enough?

Our seventy-year-old home was built at a time when the science and technology of building houses was still rudimentary. The walls' core material was massive planks of wood laid horizontally on top of each other. The outer skin was clay brick and the inner a thick layer of plaster. There was no vapor barrier or insulation in the walls and hardly any in our ceiling or that of our neighbor upstairs.

Nor did we have any of the recent technologies that contribute to energy efficiency and the prevention of heat loss. Newer heating systems, heat exchangers, and argon gas–filled triple windows and insulating products have been incorporated in new top-of-the-line houses. I'd questioned the wisdom of using such advanced gadgetry in these homes, whose sheer bulk, poor orientation, overall shape, many-angled roofs, and north-facing two-story picture windows would all distinctly offset any gains made. That January I would learn first-hand an important lesson in how common-sense design can contribute to energy savings.

There are a few basic contributors to a house's energy performance. Size is one of them. Smaller homes, unsurprisingly, take less energy to heat than larger ones. Our 1,500-square-foot (140-square-meter) home was efficiently designed and so took less energy to heat.

The building's shape is another factor. Over the past few decades the average house has not only swelled in size but its form has become more complex. Breaking with the traditional square, designers have introduced L and H shapes with a larger periphery and many more corners through which heat can leak out.

In fact, it's been found that about 15 percent less heat is lost by a rectangle-shaped house than a comparable L-shaped one. Multiple roof angles, ridges, and valleys are further places from which heat can escape and cold air can infiltrate. Despite the fact that our home had a slight extension on one end, it was basically square, which helped keep the heat in.

Houses have also become wider rather than taller in recent years; and bigger lots along with forgone attics and the addition of parking garages mean more roof area from which heat can escape without heating the floor above. Our house was taller: warm air from the basement ceiling, where the hot water pipes run, heats the main floor, even forcing us to shut off the radiator in some rooms when it gets too hot.

Whether a house is detached also affects its energy consumption. A detached home loses energy from all four facades, whereas a semi-detached has only three and a row only two (usually smaller). In an 18-by-28-foot (5.5-by-8.5-meter) plan, for example, the exterior wall area is reduced by 30 percent when two units are attached and by 60 percent when they're arranged as rowhouses. When the middle unit of a rowhouse loses heat, it goes to the neighbors. Since our home was semi-detached, at least one side of it would lose less heat.

Window quality and location further contribute to energy management. Windows are, after all, an interruption in the wall's continuity and a major source of cold air infiltration in winter and heat in summer. Window technology has made considerable breakthroughs in recent years. Flimsy wood frames with a single thin pane of glass have been replaced by sophisticated insulated aluminum or PVC frames. Double thermal glazing, sometimes filled with gas, has almost tripled the energy performance of earlier types. Well-built, energy-efficient windows are a good long-term investment in themselves, but even more so in a design for passive solar gain.

Passive solar design strategies consider the building's location, configuration, and method of construction as key factors in energy gain. Whereas active solar design requires costly mechanical means, passive solar is easier to implement if you take a common-sense approach to house design. A good orientation for a house is north–south, with the widest facade facing south. Location on the east–west axis is also acceptable, as long as the southern exposure isn't shaded by adjacent buildings.

Once the location of the building has been decided and the envelope design begun, more openings need to be arranged on the southern exposure and fewer on the northern. Gain will depend primarily on letting the sun shine through the windows and minimizing opportunities for it to escape through our colder north-side openings.

Another essential consideration involves the placement of the rooms themselves. Daytime rooms like the kitchen, living room, or family room should be placed where the sun shines to maximize the advantage of light and warmth. Night or service function rooms, like bedrooms and the laundry room, can be placed against the northern wall, since their peak hours of use are after sunset.

Creating an open plan that permits heat to travel easily from room to room and from floor to floor is also ideal. Since heat rises, having open stairs and avoiding skylights from which heat can escape will benefit the home's energy management. Once the sunlight has penetrated a room it needs to be kept there. This is accomplished by building a thermal mass—a wall located in the path of the sun to absorb the sunrise. Made of a heat-absorbent materials like masonry, the wall will release heat when the sun goes down.

I became concerned when I considered the effect of these factors on our home. The windows were older and of poor quality and many of them faced north, which meant they were likely to lose rather than gain heat. I was hoping that other design advantages would offset these losses.

The methods and practices used in the construction of a home are also critical to its performance. Super-insulated and double walls have been introduced in recent years. Most methods, unfortunately, have not made it into mainstream construction. Homebuyers, it turns out, would rather invest in expensive finishing items or fancy bathroom fixtures than in insulation. Our home was built according to old practices, yet I was surprised to find out how well it retained the heat.

When I stood in the furnace room gazing at our idle heating equipment, I felt disappointed by not having alternative means of powering the circulation pump. North Americans rely on a limited number of energy sources, the main ones being oil, coal, and hydro. In addition to not exploring the benefits of solar energy, many homeowners are unaware of a free source of energy called geothermal heat.

Geothermal energy technologies use heat from the earth for applications that range from powering a heat pump for a single home to large-scale electrical power production. In most locations, the upper 9 feet (3 meters) of the earth's surface maintains a constant temperature of between 50 and 60°F (10 and 16°C). Geothermal heat pumps can tap into this reserve to heat and cool homes. The system consists of a heat pump, an air delivery system—the ductwork—and a heat exchanger. A network of pipes is then buried in the shallow ground near the building. In the winter the pump removes heat from the exchanger and moves it into the indoor air delivery system. In the summer the process is reversed, with the pump moving heat from the indoor air into the exchanger. The heat removed from the indoor air during the summer can also be used to provide a free source of hot water.

We managed to stay three days and nights in our home, after which we moved to a friend's house. The power was restored only after nine long days had passed. It made me aware of how subjected we are to nature's mercy. When the spring finally arrived, I was happy to file the incident along with other unde-sired memories. And in case you were wondering, I also replaced all our windows with energy-efficient ones.

# A HOME IN A BOX

## THE PALMYRA

*A* large, roomy house, well designed and suitable for a corner lot, having a large front and side porch.

Details and features: Ten rooms and one and a half baths. Wraparound front porch with balcony above; bay window in dining room. Corner fireplace and sliding doors in library; built-in sideboard in dining room with colored art glass window above; open stairs.

DANNY CLEARY LOOKED TENSE AS HE WATCHED THE FIRST prefabricated wall panel rolling off the assembly line in his newly opened factory. He asked his production manager to hand him a tape measure. He carefully measured the left side of the panel, then walked around the assembly table and measured the right side and then across. "Quarter of an inch difference," he said quietly in French. "The table needs adjustment." The silence was broken by the sound of a power saw slicing lumber at the rear of the plant. Nearby, another man sorted out studs of different lengths and placed them on trolleys. From time to time he paused and looked at a computer screen attached to a pole, as if he were verifying something.

I had met Cleary a few years earlier, at another beginning phase in his career. He called me after he'd joined his father's midsize construction company. He had read about my small affordable home designs, which he persuaded his father to build. "Most buyers in our area are young, first-time homebuyers who can't afford large homes," he explained. "Your designs will suit us." His instincts were correct. Over the following few years he sold over four hundred units based on my designs and went on to become the largest builder in the region.

Cleary built his homes on site. Like most construction companies, he would subcontract out the work to a number of tradesmen, leaving himself the management. So I was a bit surprised when he called a decade later and told me about his prefabrication idea. I knew that, even for a well-off builder like him, constructing a prefab plant is a risky venture and would require a large investment. When we met, then, I asked him about the switch.

"When I visit my building sites and see a bundle of lumber delivered, thrown on the muddy soil, and watch my framers assemble it in a rainy, snowy, or hot summer day, all in the open, I sense there can be better ways to construct," he said. "Building a home in a quality-controlled, sheltered environment makes a lot of sense. I decided I could fabricate my company's own homes for less and that I could fabricate panels for other builders as well."

I was taken by Cleary's passion and vision. I was also familiar with the reality of the home-building industry, where conventional construction was paramount. Despite the obvious advantages and repeated attempts to introduce prefabrication, only 10 percent of all North American homes are built entirely in a factory. The success of factory-built homes is dismal. Over the years, they've demonstrated no economic advantage over on-site construction.

I told Cleary about the low success rate and warned him of the huge risks he was assuming. My arguments didn't seem to cool his enthusiasm. "Imagine," he said, "that we took your homes' design and streamlined their production to a small number of panels. Builders or buyers would be able to select an interior layout and we'd be able to manufacture the house using those few typical walls. It can be like the assembly of children's toy blocks!" He kept explaining to me that he'd been thinking about these ideas all along. "Besides," he confessed, "I personally want to try something new." Cleary, it seems, was determined to build his factory.

As he outlined his intentions, I recalled the three main prefabrication methods. *Modular* refers to the factory construction of sections (an entire house or part of one). The sections are hoisted into place by a crane. A *kit of parts* is another method. Well-marked individual house components (studs, windows) are shipped to the site for fabrication. The third method is to *panelize* a structure. Panels of different sizes, some with framing only (open panels) and others with insulation and windows (closed panels), are assembled according to a plan. Cleary chose a panelized system. Since walls are normally made into panels on site, panelizing doesn't constitute a radical change from conventional practice and stands a greater chance of acceptance in an industry noted for its conservative practices.

He swayed me. I agreed to be his consultant on this new venture, but I still wondered if he stood a chance of success when so many had failed. I asked myself the same questions that I had posed to Cleary. Despite huge demand, why were North American homes not built in a factory? Harsh weather, poor quality control, and high labor costs were all good reasons to build houses in a plant, yet over a million units a year are built on site. Were there *any* notable attempts to build in factories? I'd make a good start, I figured, if I learned from other efforts to introduce factory-built homes in North America. What I found out surprised me. Sears, Roebuck and Company, it turns out, had made some of the earliest prefab homes ever.

The idea of selling houses through mail-order catalogs is a strange one to many people today—but it made a great deal of sense to Sears. Although it's now a regular department store, at the turn of the twentieth century Sears sold most types of merchandise through its catalog. Comparatively few North Americans were living in cities, so Sears developed its infrastructure to serve its mainly rural clientele, providing them with everything from clothing to housing. At a time when information traveled slowly, Sears was able to reach a wide market through its catalogs. And once technology had made large-scale prefabrication and distribution feasible, introducing the sale of houses to their business was a logical step. Add to that a railroad network linking hundreds of cities and towns and the emphasis on all things modern and progressive, and the stage was set for a revolution in building technology.

Dramatic population increases at the end of the First World War created an acute need for reasonably priced, well-constructed housing that could be erected quickly. Seizing on the opportunity, Sears produced its first *Book of Modern Homes and Building Plans*. It featured twenty-two designs priced between US$650 and $2,500. Since power tools were rare and local sawmill prices could be exorbitant, pre-cut and notched lumber represented a remarkable advantage for homebuyers. Sears's two principal lines of houses, the Standard Built and the better-quality Honor Built, were sent to the site in individual pieces. This meant that the majority of Sears houses were sold pre-cut rather than fully panelized, as is the general practice today. In all cases, however, the package was complete right down to the nails. All holes were bored and millwork provided, although the carpenter on site was still expected to trim the diagonally set sub-flooring and trim and miter external sheathing. Building paper, paint and varnishes, lumber, lath, shingles, roofing, and windows were all included.

Approximately one hundred thousand Sears homes were built and sold between 1908 and 1940. The subsequent downfall of its home construction division did not result from substandard product or even poor marketing strategies. Rather, Sears's liberal financing policies failed to take into account both the possibility of economic recession and the reduced need for housing after 1924.

At about the same time as Sears ceased production, two architects from Germany began work in the United States on a factory-made house. Walter Gropius, founder of the Bauhaus, and Konrad Wachsmann developed their idea in 1941, incorporating flexibility into the design of what later became known as the Packaged House. Having received funding from private sources as well as government loans and guarantees from the National Housing Administration, Gropius and Wachsmann acquired a large war surplus factory that could produce thirty thousand houses per year.

Only a very small number of houses was produced and sold. By the 1950s the venture had collapsed, again not for technical or architectural reasons but for those related to marketing, research, and development. The competition with conventional builders of housing was too great, as the public tended to choose the most affordable options. Gropius and Wachsmann also wasted time and resources in moving the initial concept to the final production stages. They had used up half a million dollars before production began, leaving them without adequate financing. The unprofitable early years discouraged further investment, and the business dissolved for want of production capital.

Meanwhile, the massive postwar demand for housing, as well as the shortage of building materials, time pressure, and the need to build inexpensively, forced architects and builders to become innovative. Old production methods, like the placement of large horizontal pieces of wood on top of each other to construct a wall, had to be abandoned. These factors led to the modular, "stick-built" method of home construction that is used to this day.

Rather than prefabricating an entire home, pre-built products that fit in with each other took hold. Studs, for example, were spaced 16 inches (405 millimeters) apart to accommodate batt insulation of the same width, and sheets of drywall were specifically designed to fit onto the studs' center line. This assembling of different products into a seamless unit represented an exceptionally efficient method of on-site building, where the assembly of products carries on, rain or shine.

One of the companies that most exemplified this efficiency was that of William and Alfred Levitt, who introduced the wildly successful assembly-line production system. They're also attributed with the institution of power tools and labor specialization at the construction site. Self-described as the General Motors of the housing industry, the Levitts divided house construction into twenty-six carefully controlled steps. Astonishingly, an 800-square-foot (80-square-meter) house could be completed every fifteen minutes. The Levitts also produced their own nails and concrete blocks and owned lumber mills and distributing firms for electrical appliances. They strove not only to maximize the efficiency of the house construction process but also to capitalize on economies of scale.

The Long Island development where people stood in line to buy houses was dubbed Levittown—a preplanned, homogeneous mass of factory-produced housing. Between 1947 and 1951 the firm built and sold 17,447 houses in this town. The majority of their components were prefabricated en masse and assembled on site by carpenters who specialized in a particular part of the installation. Buyers could select from several facade designs for the same floor plan, and the homes were sold as a complete package with all the modern conveniences. Since the Levitts were able to buy materials and appliances at a discount, the houses came equipped with such items as built-in places for televisions, washing machines, kitchen appliances, and sliding aluminum windows. Other features designed to make a small home prestigious included a carport with outdoor storage space, additional storage space in the unfinished attic, tiled bathroom walls, flush doors, sandstone-colored bathroom fixtures (as opposed to the standard white), and bookcases built into the brick fireplace wall.

Products like plywood sheathing, roof trusses, gypsum wallboard, and aluminum siding (an offshoot of the airplane-building industry) were among the components that forever changed the way homes are put together. There has been some innovation since, but nothing that has completely overhauled these traditional, stick-built construction practices. As a builder once told me, "I'll accept any innovation that comes with twenty years of experience." Why, then, has so little changed? Unlike car manufacturing, the home-building industry is made up of small companies constructing a limited number of homes a year. The majority have few payroll employees and the work itself is subcontracted out to many trades. Taking a risk and failing can spell serious trouble for a cash-strapped firm. What might encourage a builder to take a risk? Competition. And that usually means being cheaper than the builder across the street or, in good times, delivering homes more quickly.

Another incentive for change is new market trends. Today's buyers are radically different from those in the 1940s and 1950s. More singles, and single-parent families, are buying homes. Some are looking for nontraditional layouts equipped with offices and media or exercise rooms, all of which require of builders a greater flexibility and hence innovation. So when I reflected on the next frontier in house construction and on the venture that Cleary was about to begin, I was convinced that prefabrication had not yet reached its full potential in North America. Compared with progress in the electronics and auto industries, home construction is efficient yet archaic.

Prefabrication holds the potential for higher-quality homes that are fitted to the needs of the people that occupy them. Although prefab homes are poorly regarded by the North American public, in some countries—like Sweden, where 90 percent of all homes are prefabricated—a factory-built house is a mark of comfort and quality. In Japan, where prefabs are highly esteemed, builders have joined together to create a housing show park near Tokyo. Clients visit show models and acquaint themselves with their technology and design. The next step often takes place in the client's home. A company representative sits down with the buyer and, with the aid of a computer, manipulates a generic design to make it fit the client's needs. When the design is finalized the order moves to the factory floor, where the parts are constructed by robotic equipment. Then they're shipped to the construction site for quick assembly. These prefab homes are more expensive than conventionally built ones, but the Japanese have accepted the fact that quality and choice come at a premium.

Danny Cleary worked hard to make his enterprise a success. He put aside his idea of selling and building homes like toy blocks, instead streamlining his production process and adjusting his tools. He concentrated on his core business and on the builders from the northeastern states who had become his primary clients. But two years after he began operation Cleary had to forgo the plant. He sold to his partners, who have continued the operation successfully. And Cleary himself? A few months ago he called me with another idea. But that's another story.

# A MARGARINE CONTAINER DECK

IT WAS DARK WHEN I ARRIVED AT THE PLANT. THE OLD, RUSTY-looking building loomed behind a row of tall pine trees, hidden from passing motorists en route between Montreal and Quebec City.

Light snow began to fall. I parked the car and walked to the front entrance. It was quiet and the metal door was locked. I knocked and waited. No answer. I noticed a doorbell, rang it and waited some more. The snowfall intensified, covering the ground with a thin white layer. Just as I began to wonder if anyone was inside at all, the door opened. A man wearing a blue lab coat asked me who I was. I introduced myself and he invited me to step in.

I walked into a huge space and a surreal scene. Large rectangular cubes made of countless plastic containers of all kinds formed a 30-foot (9-meter) high wall in front. When I got closer I could see yogurt cans, water and pop bottles, orange juice jugs—all made of plastic—in bales neatly held together with thin metal wires. The wall shone under the intense fluorescent light from above. No one else except my guide was in the plant.

I had come to visit the factory on the recommendation of a sponsor of the demonstration unit I was planning to construct on my university's campus. I'd become intrigued by the use of recycled domestic waste in construction materials and was wondering if the practice was at all effective in lessening the burden of our landfills or if it was merely a fancy kind of garbage collection meant to allay the concerns of a consumption-driven society. Recycling building components, like windows or toilet bowls, is common in the developing world, but what about turning household trash into building products?

"Here we begin," my host explained. "These," he said, pointing to the plastic wall, "make up the raw material that we get from sorting plants that collect them through the domestic waste recycling program in different cities." He hopped on a forklift, started its engine, and shoved its horns under the three top bales. He drove them nearby and slowly lowered them to the ground. With a metal cutter he snapped off the wires holding the cubes. Then he returned to his vehicle, lifted the bale again, and dropped it into a huge funnel-like drum. "This machine chops up the containers and melts them into resins—the plastic's original state." We walked around the machine to a large bin full of round, transparent plastic pellets. My guide pointed across and we began to walk to the other side.

"This is an extrusion element," he said. The 30-foot (9-meter) long machine featured another large container full of the pellets that I saw produced earlier. He approached a side panel and

NUTS AND JOISTS

pressed a button, whereupon the level of the pellets began to drop. As the noise grew louder a strong smell of burning plastic began to permeate the air. We walked slowly alongside the machine, whose metal arms were now moving back and forth in concert. From one end of the machine a thin, narrow, gray board began to emerge until, still smoldering, its full 10-foot (3-meter) length thudded to the floor. "Perfect," exclaimed my host with a smile. "Decking material made of recycled plastic."

From margarine containers to a construction product: it was a fascinating process. I felt that I'd witnessed a glimpse of what the future could hold. Looking at that just-produced board, I had a glimmer of hope that our environment still stood a chance. But how long will it be before such a process is widespread?

North Americans are the largest producers of solid waste in the world. It's estimated that 3.7 pounds (1.7 kilograms) of it is generated on this continent per person each day; Europeans, for example, generate half that much. We simply consume a lot, and what we buy—whether it's food, everyday household goods, or personal products—is well-wrapped. No wonder, then, that fully 33 percent of the waste generated in North America comes from residences, whereas only 30 percent comes from construction sites, 22 percent from commercial outfits, and 15 percent from industrial production.

Tending to all this waste has become a challenge and more recently a key budget item for many municipalities, primarily in urban centers. Officials simply don't know where to put it all. As landfills are stretched to capacity, garbage trucks need to drive farther and farther away to dump their smelly load. It's become a hot political and legal issue as homeowners next to landfilled sites lobby vigorously against the use of their backyards as a garbage dump. And of course there are the environmental issues. Landfills have been recognized as major polluters of groundwater, raising concerns that they're causing damage beyond their immediate location. Gases blown from landfills also have a negative effect on residents in a wider area, as has been reported in several cases.

In recent years some cities have begun to sell their waste to other towns farther away. The resulting hike in shipping costs has put further strain on municipal budgets, necessitating tax increases. Some municipalities have introduced a weight-based solid waste collection where households pay for every additional garbage bag beyond an allowed quota. Other cities have instituted regulations banning the disposal of waste containing more than 30 percent recyclable materials, forcing their citizens into the blue box program.

Domestic recycling programs have, it seems, become a natural way out of a difficult situation. They've helped reduce mounting loads in landfills and are regarded as the politically correct thing to do. Moreover, they represent the single most successful form of mass education about the environment. The once-a-week lineup of boxes at the curb is perhaps the boldest sign that average North Americans care about the long-term ramifications of human existence on the planet.

Recycling has not come cheaply. Contrary to popular belief, citizens not only contribute to waste reduction, but pay for it as well. Most programs run at a net loss. Municipalities have to cough up money to support the collection, sorting, and shipment of waste to the processing plants. The dent those programs have made in reducing piles of garbage, however, is considered worth the investment.

So what are we throwing away? The majority of our waste is fortunately made of compostable materials that decompose over time. And the rest, 32 percent, can be turned into a wide range of everyday items, construction products included.

A visit to a residential building site shows how successful recycling programs have become. It also demonstrates that builders are helping to keep the planet clean, even though it hasn't been an easy process. The products must meet such building standards as fire-rating, strength, and durability. They also have to be financially competitive with traditional products and be adopted by tradesmen and buyers alike. These products have gradually found their way into different parts of the home, but more importantly, their numbers are steadily growing.

Several of them can be found in the home's very foundation. The construction of an average wood-frame house requires some 106 cubic feet (3 cubic meters) of crushed stone under the basement slab and to cover the drainage perimeter pipes. That stone is now being replaced by crushed recycled concrete at a much lower cost. Glass, which makes up about 5 percent of domestic waste but constitutes a significant part of its volume, is similarly being crushed and applied as an aggregate for drainage. It's also used as a raw material in the production of fiberglass insulation and floor and wall tiles.

The foundation wall itself is changing. The material of choice is now polystyrene, which is used in many consumer products like meat packaging and egg cartons. The polystyrene is turned into blocks that, when put on top of each other, form a wall with a cavity into which concrete is poured. The result is an insulated foundation wall that eliminates the need to use labor-intensive wood forms and keeps the basement warm at the same time.

One of the most significant changes in house construction has been the gradual disappearance of natural wood as the prime material. Old-growth trees were traditionally used for structural lumber, but these days newly planted tree programs aren't sufficient to fill the gap that extensive harvesting has created. Although recycled wood isn't commonly used yet, manufacturers do use lower-value softwood lumber that grows more rapidly. The horizontal floor structural members—called joists—that were commonly used in past decades have been replaced by engineered trusses. These trusses are stronger than joists and are made of recycled wood chips bound together with glue. They also have a larger span, which gives the architect and the builder flexibility with their interior designs. I-joists are gradually making their way into exterior walls as well, where they replace the traditional 2-by-4 inch (5-by-10 centimeter) or 2-by-6-inch

(5-by-15 centimeter) studs. And since they're uniform, with no defects or warping, they facilitate the installation of sheeting and wallboard.

Exterior wall insulation is another area where recycled products have been making significant inroads. Here, one of the chief products used is paper, which accounts for 21 percent of domestic waste. The most common type of recycled paper is newsprint. Recycling newsprint not only decreases air pollution emissions up to 74 percent, but also uses 58 percent less water than converting virgin wood pulp to paper. It also uses up to 50 percent less energy and saves millions of trees each year. The newsprint is chopped up into small pieces, mixed with a bonding agent, and blown into the wall cavity to become an insulation buffer. Known as cellulose insulation, newsprint can replace fiberglass insulation in the roof, where it's easier to handle and install. Recycled paper can also be found in roofing paper, shingles, and the outer cover of gypsum wallboard.

Some 50 to 100 percent of new steel products contain scrap metal. This scrap was traditionally recovered from industrial waste, automobiles, and the demolition of old steel structures, but in recent years it's begun to include products from municipal solid waste. Empty tin cans put in blue boxes are turned into light-gauge steel studs that are becoming common in interior partitions. They're light, they don't warp, and electricians like them because, unlike wood studs, they don't need to drill holes in them when passing wires. The wallboard that covers the studs is, in turn, made of recycled gypsum mixed with fibers that strengthen the board. And the boards don't need a paper facing, which makes for a smoother finishing process and appearance.

Plastics, which account for 5 percent of domestic waste and 21 percent of total landfill volume, are also being sought after as a construction product. It's too expensive to reuse plastic containers for the food industry, which makes them a suitable choice for building products. Wall-to-wall interior or exterior carpets made from plastic are indistinguishable from conventional carpets, come in a range of shades and patterns, and are cost competitive. Recycled plastic can also be found right in your backyard. The plant I visited produces decking boards, outdoor handrails, street benches, and planter boxes. Outdoor stairs is just the next step.

The more than 300 million car tires that are discarded each year in North America have become the target of an intense recycling drive. These tires are a breeding ground for such disease carriers as mosquitoes and rodents, and so constitute a serious safety hazard. It's also exceedingly difficult to extinguish them in the case of fire. Recycled tires have already found their way into our driveways, sidewalks, and paths in the form of interlocking pavers, and into our living rooms as carpet underpads.

The use of products made of recycled materials has not come without a price. Some building products, interior finishings, and furnishings emit varying degrees of gases upon installation and throughout the residence. Not all products, chemicals, and odors are harmful; when the right quantities are used, they're perfectly fine. But some building products may emit gases years after they've been installed, so precautions should be taken when buying a home for sensitive occupants such as infants, older persons, and those with allergies.

It's hard to predict what the future holds for municipal recycling programs. Stockpiles of garbage in landfills across the continent *are* getting smaller, but with an average of only 10 to 20 percent of the waste recycled, we still have a long way to go. Meanwhile, many products made with recycled materials are becoming cost competitive as they gain acceptance in the marketplace. Sometime in the next decade we'll likely see a home whose components are mostly made out of recycled products. So the next time you put your blue box out, you may just find that some of its items eventually come right back into your home.

# IN PERSON

# ACCEPTING THE ORANGE TILE

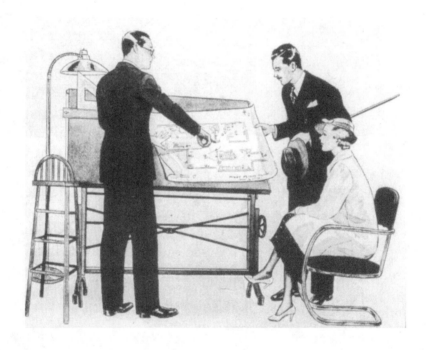

I WAS EAGER TO BEGIN MY FIRST DESIGN AS AN INDEPENDENT architect. Finally, I was on my own. There was no professor to critique my work in school or a principal instructing me how to interpret his unclear sketches at the office. It would just be my client, my ideas, and my design. So I was pretty excited on the way to the meeting with my very first clients. I thought about residences that had brought fame to their architects—Frank Lloyd Wright's 1935 Fallingwater design for Edgar J. Kaufmann in Mill Run, Pennsylvania, and Mies van der Rohe's 1950s Farnsworth House in Plano, Illinois, came to mind.

It was after dinner in July when I rang the doorbell of a modest two-story house in an established suburb. I'd been referred to my clients by an acquaintance, from whom I'd learned that they had just purchased a lot on which they wanted to have a house designed and constructed. A tall, dark-haired man in blue jeans opened the door and invited me in. At the rear I could see a kitchen table being cleared, and heard a mother instructing toddlers. Two boys and a woman appeared. "Hanna," she introduced herself. "I'm Henry," the man said. We shook hands. The boys waved and ran upstairs. Henry suggested that we sit in the living room and offered coffee.

I was wearing a suit and a tie and felt uncomfortable, but I tried to look and sound as professional as I could. I pulled out my notepad, and they began to tell me about themselves. They were both in their early thirties. Henry was a traveling sales representative for a large computer hardware company and Hanna stayed at home. They referred to themselves as a "growing family." Their young boys shared a bedroom and would soon need more space and privacy, they explained, which had triggered the building of a larger house.

As the coffee was served my questions became more specific. I asked what they wanted in their future home; for one, I needed to know what features they had in mind for their master bedroom's bathroom. This led to a discussion, among them, about bedtime and morning wake-up rituals. Hanna, I learned, usually fell asleep earlier, while Henry watched late-night TV in bed. Hanna woke up first to attend to the boys, and she liked to take a long, hot shower. The noise she made bothered Henry, who asked if something could be done about improved acoustics in their future home. The candid route that the conversation took surprised me. They had started out as strangers to me, and now we were talking about private, intimate matters.

As the evening wore on and my notepad filled up, our conversation touched on mundane aspects of home life. I asked about food storage and participation in the kitchen. When issues like these were brought up the conversation would take on a personal tone, argumentative at times, between Henry and Hanna. My architecture studies had not prepared me for such an exchange. In the house design studio at school my teachers would hand me a page outlining a house's overall area and dimensions and a very sketchy scenario of a family composition. There was nothing about daily habits, breakfasts, and holiday gatherings. I wondered what gave me the privilege of gaining access to my clients' life habits. And how would I manage to translate these discussions into brick and mortar? Home design, I quickly realized, is as much about people's lives as it is about interior layout and facade articulation.

"I forgot to show you something," Hanna said suddenly. She left the room and returned minutes later with a thick folder full of magazine cutouts. "I've been reading magazines and collecting ideas and products for years," she explained. She pulled out a page. "Here's my favorite," she said, showing me a photo of a huge, ornate fireplace. "Can you integrate this into your design?" I disliked it at first sight. This page and the others she showed me were not at all to my liking. Our tastes seemed far apart. Would I be able to work with her at all? During the course of the evening she displayed an imposing, aggressive personality. Sooner or later, I feared, we were going to clash.

She spotted my hesitation. "Anything wrong?" she asked. I felt that I had to be forthcoming with her. I admitted that I was a minimalist and that I liked simple, uncluttered spaces and designs. I also told her that I'd rather not use such products in my design. I should have brought it up earlier in the evening, I thought.

I noticed her expression change. Should I resign? There was a moment of silence. "What's wrong with simple design?" Henry asked his wife. "I can live with that." I wasn't sure if Hanna was convinced. I tried to explain that design is more than an assembly of unrelated products. There must be a unifying theme and idea, I went on. I found myself trying to articulate what architecture is in a few shallow, incoherent sentences. Would she still want me to design her home?

The practice of architecture as a formal and organized profession is relatively recent. The Industrial Revolution first introduced a need for specialized building, with office buildings and factories of all kinds demanding an in-depth knowledge of design and construction. To meet these challenges, to protect public safety, and to promote a code of ethics and formal architectural education, the American Institute of Architects was founded in 1857. Prior to that and throughout history, the design of a building was assigned to a master builder (the Greek meaning of the word *architect*), to whom skills were passed on site by an older master. The design of a building followed a pattern that had evolved over centuries and was formalized in a trial and error process. People of wealth and power were patrons of master builders; kings and clergy alike were known to commission them to design buildings that expressed their personal or national achievements or that commemorated their reign.

Over the past half-century, as the architecture profession became more institutionalized and formal, designers recognized that buildings were more than a mere enclosure for the activities that take place within them. Such background considerations as psychology and sociology—which contribute to a better understanding of inhabitants and their surroundings, be it a home or a neighborhood—were recognized as instrumental. Architects sought higher academic degrees, and university research flourished. In the mid 1970s, when I began my architectural studies, these issues expanded the architectural curriculum. The knowledge I gained in the conversation with Henry and Hanna helped me see beyond the simple design and into their lives. But I still didn't know if Hanna would engage me.

"Okay," she said finally. "I'm ready to try." Hanna returned her magazine cutouts to the folder.

I began my design by studying the building site. Consultation with zoning officials at city hall helped me figure out the required setbacks and the building types and height that were allowed. In the end, I decided to design a bungalow with a basement and a raised main floor. In order to benefit from the lot's south sunny side and in accordance with Henry and Hanna's wishes, the living room would face the street. I moved on to design the interior, referring to the notes I'd taken. Since I wasn't certain about a number of things relating to their present needs and future requirements, I drew up a list of questions to ask Henry and Hanna when we met next. Hanna, I knew, disliked basements, so I created an opening between the lower and upper floors. The fireplace, located at the lower level, could have brickwork that would extend to the upper level, helping to create physical and visual links between the two. Finally, I began to draw the house's facades, helped along with photos of the surrounding homes so that I could fit my design in with them. I wanted to distinguish the house but not alienate other residences on the street.

I was anxious when I returned to my clients' home. Would they like the concept? Would Hanna appreciate the facade's semi-modern style? Henry suggested that we sit in the kitchen. "It's cozier," he explained. Coffee was served. I unrolled the drawings and presented the designs with passion and enthusiasm, walking them through the corridors and rooms of their future home, hoping to "wow" them. They sat quietly, listening. At the end of my long presentation Hanna pointed at an architectural symbol on the plans and asked what it meant. It was a cut-out staircase connecting the two floors. I realized that she didn't read plans and could only vaguely understand the design of her new home. I learned a valuable lesson that evening: people's ability to read and comprehend architectural drawings should not be taken for granted.

Unlike the purchase of other consumer goods, homebuyers pay for a product they don't see until it's complete. And the inability to interpret designs isn't limited to clients. It takes many years of practice for architects to master the skill of visualizing how a drawn space will look once constructed. They have to foresee how much sunlight a window will let in during summer and winter months and how a certain shade of blue paint will affect a room with a particular light intensity and furniture arrangement.

Scale models and renderings are just two of the tools available to help clients visualize their unbuilt home. Computer software also allows buyers to view the design from a variety of angles. Before making a decision they can see their future house clad in such varying materials as stucco and brick. The "walk through" mode even lets buyers take a digital stroll through painted and furnished virtual rooms.

I explained what the symbol was. Henry said that he liked the design, and that he appreciated the openness of the layout. Hanna was more reserved. "Something's missing," she said, without pointing to any one aspect in particular. They started to ask more detailed questions and made additional comments.

I was puzzled by the arguments and disagreements between them. When I found myself refereeing I felt as though I'd been unwillingly drawn into a side-taking dance. Hanna stood her ground. When it came to home life issues she ignored her husband's ideas, saying, "What do you know, you're never here anyway." Henry insisted on demonstrating his technical knowledge. When I referred to acoustics, wall and ceiling insulation values, and window types, he'd become visibly alert.

It was late at night when I finally left. I felt lucky; they hadn't dismissed my basic ideas. Still, my plans were full of notes and suggestions. I was instructed to make amendments, get their final approval, and move on to the preparation of construction documents.

Hanna insisted on participating in all stages of the design. She wanted to have a say in every detail: what size the windows would be, and where in the room they'd be placed. At the time, I even felt that I'd lost an opportunity to design the house I wanted, one that would find its way into the fame of glossy magazines. Henry was the blank-check type of client, the kind who let me do whatever I wanted and was willing to go along with any of my ideas as long as they were within reason and budget. He gave me a free hand to select finishes and trusted my suggestions and taste.

Construction on Henry and Hanna's home began in the fall when a building permit was issued, a builder selected, and a contract signed. Since I'd been asked to supervise construction, I visited the building site regularly to make sure that my plans were followed correctly and to ensure good workmanship. I also accompanied my clients on site visits and explained the work's progress.

One early morning during construction Hanna called. She said she'd visited the site that morning alone and had decided she wanted to do without the opening between the lower and upper floors. She feared, she said, that the noise from the lower level would disrupt life on the upper. My heart sank. I immediately knew that her suggestion would alter the entire design concept. I also knew that at this late stage she'd have to pay a hefty monetary penalty since the rough carpenters who had built the frame had finished their work and begun construction elsewhere.

Bringing them back would be costly. But Hanna kept making more arguments about visual effect, which I tried my hardest to counteract. At times our conversation came close to a heated argument. We finally agreed to take the evening to reflect before my telephone call to the builder the next morning.

An architect or client changing their mind during construction is common. Despite the advantages that illustrative tools provide, the end product—the built home—is often different from the envisioned images. It's hard to know whether a proportion chosen for a family room will make it cozy or oversized. There are several critical phases during construction in which an intervention can be made and changes performed on the design of a home. Placing the interior wall studs is one such stage. Examining the spaces at this point provides a concrete sense of how each room will feel. The cladding of the home's interior with gypsum boards is another indication of the space's proportions. Once plumbing pipes and electrical wires have been passed through the walls it's more expensive to change the room's configuration since several trades must be recalled. Builders try to discourage clients from changing their mind, then, as it will disrupt a carefully planned sequence of tasks.

The next morning Hanna called. She told me that after much discussion and debate with Henry she had decided to keep the opening and the two-story fireplace arrangement. I told her that I felt she'd made a good decision. She reminded me that we had to begin selection of finishes: tiles, carpets, and shades of paint.

I suggested that I prepare a sample of what might be suitable and show it to her.

I dreaded that stage. People's tastes are so varied. How could we agree on so many things? And my track record with Hanna was not in my favor.

Decorating a home isn't an easy task; it's a process that develops by accretion, through trial and error and adaptation to the twists and turns of our life at different times. Based on both intuition and experience, the process may evolve every year or even every season. People seldom get things right on the first try; it often takes years until they reach a satisfying level of domestic comfort. Meanwhile, though, those tiles and wall-to-wall carpets had to be chosen.

Hanna didn't like the rationale of my color choices, nor the samples I'd brought with me. They were too "artsy," she said, and lacked the boldness she was looking for. We decided to visit several stores to see a wider selection, and spent hours matching tiles and carpets. Eventually I got tired and restless and Hanna offered to continue on her own. I knew that my design was at stake; that her choices could well destroy the essence of what I was trying so hard to create. Besides, I particularly hated the orange tile she'd chosen for the kitchen. I insisted on staying.

In early spring, Henry and Hanna and their two boys moved into their new home. It was a modest house nestled among similar homes on a quiet street. In the end I realized that, more than creating a grand design, I had translated their personal needs and aspirations into brick and mortar. Despite my uneasy, often rocky relations with Hanna, I appreciated her perseverance and insistence on getting the home she wanted. When she walked people through its hallways and rooms she felt a sense of ownership and pride. The home, I knew, wouldn't earn me acclaim or find its way into the pages of glossy magazines. It would be, however, a comfortable place for a family. My clients were happy. Hanna got the orange tile that I hated so much, and Henry had an acoustic wall for his sound system.

# BEAULIEU'S RACE

MARCEL BEAULIEU WAVED HIS HANDS AND SIGNALED TO THE driver of the moving truck to stop when it reached the edge of the loading dock of the Diexpo exhibition hall in Guadalajara, Mexico. An unshaven, tired-looking Mexican driver stepped down out of his cab and climbed onto the dock. Beaulieu approached him, pointed to his watch, and began an angry conversation in broken Spanish. The driver matched Beaulieu's tone of voice and waved his hands as if to say that he wasn't at fault. They abruptly ended the shouting match and headed to the truck's back cargo doors.

Together they cut the metal seal that the Mexican border agents had put on the door. Beaulieu looked tense as he glanced at his watch and nodded his head as if to acknowledge that he'd lost precious time in a race that was about to begin. It was 3 p.m. on a Tuesday in November. Three days later, on Friday at 10 a.m., Beaulieu was scheduled to attend a ribbon-cutting ceremony of a house whose components were packed in the truck's narrow container, a house that he was about to construct.

Beaulieu feared that overzealous Mexican customs agents, whose integrity was rumored to be questionable, might have tampered with the truck's valuable contents. He was eager to find out whether the cargo that had left his warehouse in East End Montreal had made it intact to Guadalajara.

I had been introduced to Beaulieu six months earlier. He and his son, Pierre, owned a small company that manufactured prefabricated wall panels. I'd been looking for someone to build a prototype of a low-cost home that I'd designed for the Guadalajara ConstruExpo Home Show. The 500-square-foot (46-square-meter) unit, dubbed La Casa a la Carta, was to be produced in Canada and assembled in Mexico. It was meant to showcase Canadian construction products, and the companies' representatives would be on site during the three-day fair to promote them.

The metal doors opened with a scratching sound. Beaulieu, with his hand angled over his glasses to better see into the container's dark belly, stepped in and touched the panels as if to verify that they'd really arrived. He'd been anxious all day. The trucking company had assured him that the truck would arrive sometime early on Tuesday morning, and its late arrival meant that he'd lost almost an entire working day. He feared that this chunk of lost time would haunt him later and that he'd have to rework his entire schedule.

Beaulieu and his son were accompanied by two laborers, Mathieu and Gilles, who had arrived with them from Quebec. The trip was organized and managed by a company who profited by linking Canadian manufacturers with Mexican distributors. A handful of other people were therefore on hand to unload the container and put the products inside the exhibition hall where the house was to be assembled.

It wasn't until 7 p.m. that the unloading ended. Some team members decided to retire for the night. In one of the hall's corners, meanwhile, Beaulieu stood surrounded by Pierre, Mathieu, and Gilles. Pierre, who held an engineering degree, unfolded a piece of paper and explained that, according to his calculations, they'd make up the lost time only if construction commenced at once and continued through the night. Beaulieu dismissed the plan, saying that they'd be exhausted in the following days. He suggested that they work as late as they could and then get some sleep.

Despite Beaulieu's enthusiasm about the project and his well-meaning spirit, I had some reservations. He was a manufacturer and lacked experience in assembly. Completing a home in three days would be an awesome challenge, even for an experienced builder. He and his crew would have to perform the tasks of many tradespeople, and some of those tasks required skills they did not possess. Would the house be ready for the visiting dignitaries on Friday morning? To speed things along I simplified the design of the prototype as much as I could. Except for its lack of foundation and plumbing it was no different from any other house of the same size, the conventional construction of which would normally take about two full years in Mexico.

I wanted to demonstrate that construction times could be significantly shortened by streamlining the process and prefabricating the building, but would it be possible to reduce it to a mere three days?

The crew began by marking the house's location on the cement floor and then building a wooden platform made of joists covered with plywood. Then came the exterior wall panels. Two men lifted each of the 8-by-15-foot (2.4-by-4.6-meter) sections as they were placed at right angles to each other and connected by metal fasteners. As more panels were added, the square shape of the house began to emerge. It was 1 a.m. Beaulieu, who was sweating, stopped his work and opened a can of pop. Sixty years old and silver-haired, he wore a special belt around his waist to protect his back from heavy lifting. He took a long sip from his can, then called to his team. He suggested they call it a day.

Beaulieu was an innovator of sorts; his past experiences included many attempts to develop or distribute new products. In an industry known for its conservative practices, he was an oddball. Several years earlier he'd come across a technology that he firmly believed had the potential to cure the housing shortage in the developing world. The product, which he further developed, was a panel made of thin, lightweight cement sheets affixed to either side of a wood or metal frame. To the void in between Beaulieu injected chemical liquids that, when mixed and hardened, formed the thermal barrier that lent the panel its rigidity and lightness.

He proposed that the panel's low cost, along with its thermal properties and the light weight that eliminated the need for heavy machinery to erect it, made it particularly suitable for mass production in the developing world. Like other inventors I'd met over the years, Beaulieu was sure he'd developed a cure-all product. But he still had to build the house to prove his point, and time was short.

Beaulieu and his team arrived at the building site at 7 a.m. They stood a short distance from the enclosure they had completed the night before, sipping coffee from Styrofoam cups. They had ahead of them two full days and nights to complete the building. The house still didn't have a roof, interior partitions, and, of course, any of the finishings. I approached the group and greeted them. Then, when I looked at the building's side elevation, I immediately noticed an error. The window opening on one of the bedroom panels was smaller than what I'd specified, a mistake that must have been made in Beaulieu's plant where the panels were produced. It meant that the window itself, which was produced according to the true measurements, wouldn't fit the opening. The panel could be cut and the opening enlarged, but more time would be lost. I had no choice but to break the bad news to them. It would be a bad start for a long day.

Beaulieu was upset. He immediately approached Pierre, who had supervised the panel's production in Montreal, and scolded him for neglecting to verify the window opening size. He assured me that the error would be corrected before Friday. Given the time left, I had doubts that it could be done at all.

The work went on. Roof panels, similar to the ones used in the wall and supported by the interior partitions installed earlier on, were lifted up and placed across the 15-foot (4.6-meter) span. A large wooden beam was then placed across the front of the structure above the combined kitchen, living, and dining space.

The interior layout was the outcome of a scenario that was created for an imaginary housing project. I envisioned a young family buying a first-time home in a low-cost, perhaps social housing development. The family, made up of working parents and two children aged four and two, would visit a demonstration site where they saw several model homes and a menu of interior components. Based on their budget and space requirements, they would make their selections. The design would let them expand the house progressively—both horizontally and vertically—to accommodate a larger family, house a live-in relative, or supplement their income by renting out a room.

At noon the bare structure was complete. Panels were placed along the roof perimeter to form a parapet. It started to resemble the house I'd envisioned, but there was still a long way to go. The time spent on finishing a home is much longer than building its raw structure. I knew, however, that from this stage on many tasks could proceed in parallel. The work could be carried out by

Beaulieu's team as well as by the representatives who accompanied their products. I didn't know, though, if the small home would have room for them all. Beaulieu and his crew broke for lunch.

After lunch the team split, with Beaulieu and Pierre working on the interior while Mathieu and Gilles began to clad the exterior with stucco. Covering a house with stucco is hard manual labor. Two layers have to be placed: one that smoothes out the surface and covers the panel's joints, and another—the final one—that gives the exterior its final shade and texture. It would also have to be painted, and for this I had selected a combination of light gray and blue similar to some of the colors I'd noticed on Mexican homes during earlier visits. Mathieu and Gilles, who had a day and a half to complete the task, decided that Mathieu would work on the exterior while Gilles would plaster the interior, preparing it for painting as well. I wondered if they'd get around to fixing the window at all.

The afternoon marked a new phase in the life of the project. The gray structure began to resemble a home as windows and doors were installed. A local electrician arrived. Beaulieu explained to him that plastic conduits had been placed in the wall panels during their fabrication. Through them, he said while demonstrating, wires had to be fished and connected to receptacles. Accompanied by his young assistant, the electrician surveyed the house. He returned moments later and began to haggle with Beaulieu about a price. More waving of hands ensued, but they finally shook on it. I breathed a sigh of relief: we might not have a finished house, but at least we'd have light.

It was time to begin the flooring. I had chosen linoleum for the house's front and hallway with a pattern that combined different shades. Mark, a representative of the manufacturer, arrived to install it. He smeared the floor's plywood with epoxy, to which he affixed long layers of the linoleum that he cut from a roll.

It was dinnertime when the work stopped. Beaulieu and his team looked exhausted; Mathieu and Gilles were covered with spots of plaster from head to toe. They all sat quietly on paint cans. Gilles smoked. As Julie, a representative of the company that organized the show, handed them cans of soda and sandwiches, the sense of despair was palpable. In my mind I went through a long list of items that still needed to be completed, trying to match them with the time remaining. The kitchen cabinets and the bathroom fixtures still had to be installed, a labor-intensive, time-consuming process. I began to think about contingency plans. I found myself writing an imaginary script, an explanation of sorts for the visiting dignitaries on Friday.

Beaulieu avoided looking at me. He began to blame the trucking company for the delay, saying that he would never, ever engage them again in any of his projects. It was clear that any hope of having some rest during the night would have to be scrapped. Productivity after two long working days and one night would also drop to a minimum. There was no choice, though, but to venture into the night and hope for a breakthrough, or perhaps a miracle.

Fall is pleasant in Guadalajara, neither too hot nor too cold. I stepped out into the sunny street outside the exhibition center. A new day began. Honking motorists passed by and children laughed and cheered on their way to school. I was tired, my body ached, and I badly needed a shower. I stepped back into the exhibition hall and sat on a pile of cement board. Pierre lay on the ground next to me, sleeping. Beaulieu sat holding his head, his eyes closed. Mathieu and Gilles lay on the floor behind me, awake. It was quiet.

Suddenly, somebody yelled Beaulieu's name from afar. He opened his eyes, searching in the distance. The call was repeated. A man approached us, looking tiny in the vast exhibition space. Beaulieu jumped to his feet and ran toward him. The two hugged each other as the team members rose to their feet cheering. The man introduced himself: Guy worked for Beaulieu. He'd been unexpectedly called as a witness in a court case, which held him in Montreal. When the case was dismissed he was let go, so he took advantage of the airline ticket he'd already bought and decided to join his boss in Guadalajara. He had arrived the night before.

The project received an unexpected jolt of energy that morning. Beaulieu showed Guy around the project. They decided that Guy's first task would be to enlarge the opening and install the missing window. Representatives of the kitchen and bathroom fixture suppliers appeared sometime later. They began to unwrap the bulky packages and prepare their contents for installation.

The day had the markings of a feverish race against time. Many people were trying to work in each free corner of La Casa's interior, narrowly missing one another as they brought in materials and tools. The noise was tremendous. People spoke to each other in English, French, and Spanish. Walls were painted, bathroom floors tiled, light fixtures installed, kitchen cabinets leveled, moldings painted.

At 9 p.m. a truck loaded with furniture arrived. A local Mexican architect named Guadalupe Dipp Reyes, who had been engaged to furnish the home's interior, accompanied the truck. She brought with her a team of helpers who began to unload the vehicle. By midnight I was exhausted. I realized that being there wasn't helping me or the project. I needed sleep. Beaulieu and his crew decided to follow me, hoping that the house would be ready by the next morning.

I woke up at 9 a.m., not knowing what day it was. It immediately dawned on me that an hour later the ribbon-cutting ceremony inaugurating La Casa a la Carta would take place. Was the house ready, clean, and furnished? I rushed to the site.

The Honorable Alberto Cardenas Jiménez, governor of the state of Jalisco, arrived at the house at 10:15 a.m. accompanied by an entourage of dignitaries representing the city, the state, and the country. The house stood sparkling clean, waiting to begin its life as an idea that would one day offer low-income Mexicans their first home. In a country with a yearly housing shortage estimated at 700,000 units, our race demonstrated that it's possible to accelerate the building process. It's within that country's reach to provide the poor with well-built homes they could be proud to own. Beaulieu and his crew were there to witness the ribbon-cutting ceremony. They were all dressed up, tired but proud.

# OUR FIRST HOME

I LIKED THE WEEKEND VISITS TO OPEN HOUSES WHEN MY WIFE and I were looking to buy our first home. As real estate agents walked us through the property, invariably overstating its qualities, I would take a peek at the decor. Photos on the walls and mementos in glass cabinets always drew my attention. I would imagine what I'd do with the place if I became its owner. How would I remodel it to suit our family's needs? When, later in the day, we returned to our apartment, we'd carefully study the property's listing page and calculate what the monthly mortgage would be and whether or not we could afford it.

Shortly before our wedding, we had rented the spacious second floor of a duplex on a quiet residential street. We considered ourselves fortunate. Built in the 1930s, the apartment had tall ceilings, oak moldings, and maple wood floors. We each had a large study, as we were completing our degrees. When our daughter was born we gave up one of the studies. We converted the second study when our son was born two years later.

The pressure began to build. We had a number of ideas about how to renovate and make better use of the space, but we knew there was no sense in investing in a property that wasn't ours.

And then there was the monetary pressure: paying monthly rent did not bring us any closer to home ownership. So we set a financial target, found out how much we'd be allowed to borrow based on our modest earnings, and began looking for a house within that range.

Choosing the right home, primarily the first one, is ranked among life's hardest decisions. For most households, the choice will have long-term ramifications on financial status, family planning, and physical comfort. It's a complex process that often involves striking a balance and making tradeoffs between several key aspects. Family size, and its members' ages, education, ethnicity, and income are all critical. Some buyers, for instance, search for a house that will raise their social status, or one that's near their own family, ethnic group, or faith.

The home itself represents another group of influencing aspects. Its asking price, its age, the number of bedrooms, the type of heating system, and maintenance costs are among the factors there. Neighborhood-related issues include travel distance to work, school, and shopping, property tax value, and the proximity of public parks. And then there's the question of how long the buyers want to live in the place. Will a new job prospect elsewhere sway them to sell, or are they planning to stay long regardless?

When people begin their search for a home they prioritize these aspects. Some issues are given priority, while others fall to the bottom of the list. As they begin the quest, market reality sets in and the initial order of priorities begins to shift. They soon realize that earlier assumptions were unrealistic and need to be adjusted. They trade off one aspect for another. When affordability becomes a consideration, a desire to live in an old, expensive home a short distance from work will be traded for a new home in a tract development with a longer traveling distance.

My wife and I wanted to live in an old neighborhood, and we set our sights on one in particular. The vintage brick-clad homes, the old-fashioned commercial street a walking distance away, and the tall trees were enough to convince us to abandon the idea of living in the burbs. The reputable kindergarten and elementary school nearby was another tilting factor. We spent many weekends searching, unable to accommodate what we liked within our budget. The pressure continued to build. Our daughter would reach school age the next year and we wanted to register her in that school. To our misfortune, however, it was also a vendor's market.

The mid-1980s saw the first of the baby boom generation acquiring their homes. The boomers, on average, had more money to spend on housing than their parents' generation. Some were supported financially by their parents. From that time until the early 1990s real estate prices rose rapidly in most North American urban centers. Interest rates, a result of an out-of-control economic spiral, also mounted and reached 15 percent. It was not, in short, the right time to buy. We knew our mortgage payments would be excessively high and would affect our finances for years to come. So back and forth we would go: put our homeownership hopes aside for a while, or just take the plunge?

A friend called one Friday night, telling us that she'd just seen a For Sale sign put on the lawn of a house in a street that we liked and had repeatedly visited. A week earlier, a house of the kind we were searching for was sold on that very same street. We knew about the sale and regretted not being more decisive and risk-taking, blaming ourselves for missing a splendid opportunity to own our first home. We were eager not to miss a chance this time around.

We called the vendor's agent and arranged a visit for the following day. On a cold Saturday afternoon in February, the agent waited for us in front of the house. Unable to make babysitting arrangements, we brought our young children along. The owner, a serious-looking old woman, opened the door. It was a two-story, brick-clad house with an unfinished basement attached on the south side to another, similar home. The vendor lived on the main level, with a rental unit on the second floor. It dawned on me that if we bought the house we'd have to become landlords, a responsibility we didn't want at all.

We whisked through the house quickly, not taking the time to carefully appreciate and inspect the place. Our tired son began to cry in my arms. I noticed a number of fine architectural details that lent the house an old-fashioned appeal that we liked so much, but more recent modifications were plain and banal. My intuitive impression was that the place had potential and that a great deal of work and money were needed to make it truly nice. In our haste we took only a superficial look at the basement and agreed to visit the upper floor later.

We stepped out to a breezy day accompanied by the vendor's realtor. The tall, slim, dark-haired woman spoke English with a thick French accent. She asked us what we thought of the place. We suggested that we meet in our apartment in about an hour.

We were tense on our drive home. Our son fell asleep in his seat, and our daughter kept reciting a children's song. We knew we'd have to make a quick decision, something that we both hated. We felt that if we weren't decisive, an opportunity would be lost once again. I tried to recall the home's interior. It had potential, yet we were far from falling in love with it at first sight. The asking price was also very high: we'd have to stretch our financial means to the limit. Were these parts of the tradeoff that we'd have to make?

Unlike cars, homebuyers can't test-drive a home before moving in. They can't live in it for a while and then make up their minds. They can only hope that their instincts, intuition, and experience will serve them well. While most people approach their search with a well-organized list of priorities, their rationale often collapses in the face of something they hadn't considered. Whether it's a tempting kitchen, a fully loaded bathroom with convenient fixtures, a spacious, well-landscaped backyard, attractive interior woodworking details, or a tall ceiling that tips the scales, the final decision involves passion as much as logic.

We arrived back at our apartment. The realtor followed shortly thereafter, and we sat in the dining room and served coffee. In a soft voice she told us that the vendor, the serious-looking old lady, a widow, was interested in moving upstairs and becoming our tenant. In return for renovating the unit at her own expense, she'd like to sign a ten-year rental lease.

The offer confused us even more. My intuitive reaction was positive. A guaranteed rental income for ten years would ensure a bank loan. We wouldn't have to worry about finding a tenant, and wouldn't have to spend money, which we didn't have much of, on renovating the upper unit. On the other hand, I didn't know much about our vendor. What would happen if the relationship between us went sour? After the realtor told us the rent the woman was offering, we calculated the monthly mortgage payment, trying to figure out if we were within our spending limit.

People commonly stretch themselves financially when they buy their first home. In their calculations they follow a formula put forward by their banker. They're allowed to borrow the equivalent of 32 percent of their household income for what financial institutions call "shelter allowance." That sum includes mortgage payments, municipal taxes, and heating expenses. But buyers often tend to ignore other things like legal fees, moving costs, and decorating expenses. They'll have to buy furniture and window blinds, and there are always unforeseen maintenance costs. Those who buy a home a long distance from their workplace may have to buy a second car, as both heads of the family will likely have to continue working in order to meet the mortgage payments. Things can get hectic for families with toddlers, what with daily stops at the daycare before and after work. Many also begin a round of remodeling.

Studies show that most financial adjustments take place within the first three years following occupancy. That 32 percent of a combined household income allowed for borrowing soon turns into 50 percent as the new homeowners spend additional sums of money. As a result, first-time homebuyers often become financially strained shortly after moving in.

My wife showed me the calculator after a long process of number-crunching that included several scenarios. In all of them we were over our monthly spending limit. It came to decision time. The realtor asked us what we had decided. In her soft voice she argued that it was an amazing deal. "The deal of the century," she called it. She hinted that if we declined to buy she'd get in touch with another couple, clients of hers who were desperate to find a home in the area. She was certain they'd "grab it." It might even turn into a bidding war if we were to change our minds later; a war, she predicted, we were destined to lose.

My wife and I asked for some private time. We went to the master bedroom where we began an intense discussion. Many for and against arguments were exchanged. Ultimately, though, we just didn't want to lose another opportunity to become homeowners. We returned to the dining room and signed an Offer to Purchase form, conditional on the bank's approval of our application to mortgage and a positive outcome of a building inspection.

The realtor commended us and left to have the vendor accept our offer and sign. She couldn't predict the outcome, she said, but if she got a signature she'd return that evening. It was a long and nerve-racking wait. Two hours later the doorbell rang. The realtor congratulated us, saying that we had got ourselves a home. She handed us a copy of the signed offer and promised to call the next day to discuss additional formalities.

I hugged my wife.

It was past midnight when we went to bed. I couldn't fall asleep. I continually replayed the events of that Saturday afternoon. Had we been too hasty? It occurred to me that I'd neglected to consider many issues that we'd regarded as essential. Did I really want to undertake such an overwhelming remodeling job? Would we have any funds left once we bought the place? I also agonized over the fact that I had negotiated poorly. The vendor probably noticed us rushing through her home with our kids; she must have known how eager we were to buy. There had been hardly any negotiation to speak of. Then there was the very high interest rate. Was this the right time to buy at all? We could have waited for a better economic climate, a buyer's market perhaps, saving ourselves a fortune.

When the day broke after a long night of no sleep and mulling things over, I decided to get out of the contract I'd signed the night before. I was even willing to lose the small deposit we'd made. When my wife woke up I shared my thoughts with her. She disagreed but said she'd support me if this was how I felt. I phoned a lawyer I knew, who told me that I had no recourse. I'd signed a binding legal document that had to be respected. The offer would be considered void only if our request for a loan wasn't approved by a bank—something that I already knew wouldn't happen—or if a major structural defect was found in the inspection.

Despite being an architect, I did not possess the skills necessary to conduct a building inspection. Inspectors know how to read stains on a ceiling or cracks in the foundation walls, signs that reveal information about the building's condition. From a colleague I got the telephone number of an experienced inspector, and arranged to meet him at the house the following day. When we met I was struck by how well organized and energetic he was. As he began his inspection, I once more agonized over the fact that many of the things I was about to see would be for the first time. I should have been more thorough in my first visit. Deep in my heart I was hoping he'd find a structural defect that would get me out of the signed contract.

He conducted a thorough inspection which I accompanied. He climbed on top of the flat roof, verifying its condition. He carefully walked around the foundation, hunting for cracks and meticulously writing notes in his pad. He surveyed the brick and the brick joints for signs of crumbling or a weakened wood frame behind. Inside he paid careful attention to every crack in the wall, explaining to me their causes and taking more notes. He examined the house plumbing and the electrical system. It all seemed fine. Then we went down to the lower level. He took a look at the old gas furnace, commented that it would have to be replaced sometime soon, further agonizing me. The exposed foundation walls were painted green and seemed sound. In one corner was a neatly packed row of firewood arranged parallel to the wall. We were about to leave when he suggested we verify what was behind it. He moved some of the logs. A crack was revealed. I quickly began to remove more logs. A 10-foot (3-meter) long crack became visible on the foundation wall between the home I was about to buy and the neighbor's. I'd finally found the hook I was so desperately looking for. As we left the house the inspector told me that he'd type up his report and fax it to me the next day.

I returned home and shared his findings with my wife. We weighed our options and carefully mulled over the procedure necessary to get out of our signed contract. I didn't sleep much that night. I knew that the inspector would only record the findings, and that it was up to me to write a letter arguing that I had discovered a major structural defect, one that rendered our agreement null and void.

*Would* the crack in the foundation be recognized as a major structure defect by the vendor? She could engage her own expert who might dispute my claim. The process could be entangled in the courts for a long time. But I had to ask myself whether I was simply fearing the implications of becoming a homeowner, of committing myself to the risks and undertakings that every business deal entails. Was I using a crack that most foundations in houses of this age would have to get out of the contract? In other words, was I getting cold feet?

In July we took possession of the home. The vendor moved in to the renovated upstairs unit. Our relations were cordial. Our place underwent extensive renovations over the years, fitting it to our changing needs. The acquisition has proven to be a good investment. We've seen the value of our property rise. But most of all, it's been a comfortable place for our family.

# DESIGN FOR FAMILY LIFE

"FRIDGES SHOULD BE MANUFACTURED WITH EXPANDABLE doors," my wife suggested one evening as she tried to affix a note with a magnet to the crowded surface of our refrigerator. As two very busy academics with two active teenagers, managing time in our home requires an almost military efficiency. We're endlessly trying to catch up with one another's schedules. Driving the kids to school and after-school sports and social activities, respecting community and social obligations, attending medical appointments and parent–teacher interviews, keeping up with household chores like grocery shopping and laundry pickup—altogether, it doesn't seem to leave time for much else.

Our home sometimes resembles a train station, with family members and friends coming and going and reminding each other when and where they have to be met or picked up. Cellphones play a crucial role as the acrobatic task of changing meeting places is, at times, done from the road. And when we're all at home things don't seem to get any easier or slower, given the constant need to catch up with work or study obligations in the process of preparing for tomorrow's class or meeting at the office. We each have a private domain where we try to finish our never-ending tasks.

Eventually, I realized that I was whisking through some of life's events too quickly. I began to regard time as a commodity, and that the time spent with my family is precious. I paid greater attention to quality of time. I even tried to find answers within the realm of my profession, design, to the challenges I faced at home.

As an architect I often ask myself whether home design can facilitate better family relations. It is no doubt part of the larger question as to whether good or bad architectural design can influence behavior. As an architecture student in the 1970s, I recall debating the issue. Some argued that properly designed buildings and communities can make their inhabitants friendlier or even reduce crime. Others suggested that it's really a stretch to expect architecture or architects to become behavioral modifiers.

I support the notion that people's behavior can't be easily distinguished from the environment in which it occurs. Be it a single home or a neighborhood, the outcome of a design project is above all where encounters between people take place. A large room with poor acoustics is, in my view, a bad choice for an intimate conversation, for example. Similarly, a low-density neighborhood with big garage doors, wide boulevards, and no sidewalks, trees, lampposts, or benches isn't a pleasant place for people to meet. But I'm still left pondering the role of the home itself—its layout and its decor, and the opportunities they provide for interaction among the people who live there.

Today's increasing pressure on the family schedule is a result of several factors, among which is, paradoxically, the home itself.

The gradual expansion in the size of homes and their amenities in the 1970s drove their prices up and necessitated two incomes for their purchase and maintenance. The return, en masse, of women to the labor force restructured household responsibilities and priorities. The family's basic daily chores now had to be compressed into the weekend and a smaller number of weekday hours. Every time slot before the beginning and end of a workday had to be taken advantage of. Mom was simply not there full-time to look after household necessities.

A high standard of living and its never-ending spiral of consumption haven't allowed many households to reverse course. North Americans are in debt, and two pay checks are needed to keep afloat. The 1990s recession years saw companies become highly efficient through automation and layoffs. Workloads grew and the number of payroll employees shrank. Work not completed during regular work hours had to be done after hours at home. The internet made it even more tempting to put aside family responsibilities and focus on work. Every household member began to go online in their own room or study.

The rising standard of living has also meant more recreational opportunities. Recreation has gone from spontaneous to organized and regimented activity: parents exercise at the gym while the young play soccer and hockey in leagues with schedules rather than in the backyard or the street in front. More time is often spent preparing for and getting there rather than on the activity itself.

In recent years the layouts of homes have made them thoroughly public places. A great number of intimate and private places have been lost. The transformation took place when, in the name of style, convenience, or space savings, functions were combined and the open-plan concept thrived. The living room was merged with the dining room; the family room became part of the kitchen. The space that has seen the greatest decline in intimacy is the bedroom, where a TV/DVD set has become an indispensable feature. Quiet time for reading or conversation that was once part of the ritual of changing gears at the end of a hectic day is now filled with more electronic appliances instead.

So how does one make use of the few precious minutes that we do have to spare for a family get-together during the day? It can start by altering family behavior, by reshaping priorities and placing human relation at the top of the list. And proper design can help. It begins by establishing comfortable spaces in which family members can sit together. A cozy dining area adjacent to the kitchen, for example, is conducive to pleasant talks about the coming day, once it's been decided that breakfast in common is important. Having it properly lit, with a serving counter nearby so that everyone can remain seated, can make a difference. In the very same space dinner can take place to the sound of soft music. Alternatively, families can revive their old forgotten dining room and eat there daily. Similarly, a sunroom can be used year round as an extension of the kitchen, with enough space to relax after dinner in one another's company. Decks also help foster an informal mood and cement a team spirit with everyone taking part in preparing and serving a meal.

Family rooms have experienced ups and downs in recent years; today they're more apt to be used by families with toddlers or young children. When children are older, however, the family room can be reconfigured as a reading room, a space where household members can read in the old-fashioned way—in the company of others, and without competing with the sound of a television. Walls of books, comfortable couches, and a soft rug would make this a pleasant gathering space. The hobby room is another space that, over the years, has faded from the residential vocabulary. Whether it's in the basement or an area near the bedrooms, it can be a place where family members work together on a school project or assemble a multi-piece toy or jigsaw puzzle.

The home's decor and accessories can also be made to foster strong family relations by serving as a reminder of roots and times past. When I visit the homes of acquaintances for the first time and follow along on a room-by-room tour, I often regard the place as a family album. I pause in the hallway and examine a grandparent's faded photo, looking for similarities between the image and my hosts. I stop at a family room and spot childhood photographs of my friends, their wedding and vacations on a sandy beach. I'm curious to know what they looked like in their youth, and I'm intrigued by what I see in the background. At times I ask questions and want to find out their relation to the people posing. Graduation photos are my favorite; people look genuinely happy in them. I also like to ask about mementos in a glass cabinet. People's eyes light up when I spot something they're really fond of or that reminds them of a special place or time. There's often a story attached, which my hosts encourage each other to tell.

As I make my way through rooms I walk through time. It's not a house I'm traversing, but a life: the recorded memory of moments, days, and years of the people who live there. Homes, I concluded when I began to design, are as much about memories and aspirations as they are about walls and shades of paint. The choice and mounting of a family photo is a significant act; it's of a different order altogether than that of mounting an artwork. Whereas art is a reflection of a family's likes, moods, or wealth, a memento found in a faraway bazaar is a reminder of the trip that took them there. My hosts are often eager and proud to show me an acquired piece of art, and yet they tend to rush through the art of life itself.

How does one create a museum of life? By recording. Memories worth recording are created at home all the time. One needs, of course, to know what to keep, and how and where to display it. A child's first shaky sketch may seem unimportant at the time, but years later that drawing may be a telling representation. Objects and scale are all authentic reflections of who we were. Parents can create a portfolio of their children's work, to be taken out and looked at from time to time. A particularly evocative piece or a collage of work from different ages can be framed or laminated and mounted.

Creating a wall full of photos is another meaningful act. Hallways, stairways, and bedroom bureaus are all good places for then-and-now framed photos. And then there are electronic recordings—labeled, ideally, and kept in an appropriate place. Video recorders and digital cameras are commonly used to capture moments with children; it may be time to record parents and their stories before it's too late. A recorded casual conversation can become a priceless artifact.

Clothing is an important part of the family's memory lane. Brides tend to keep their wedding gowns, and parents cherish baby's first outfit. Furniture can likewise be treasured: a chest of drawers, a framed mirror, a hallway entrance bureau may all evoke memories. Old china and utensils should be displayed, if possible, in a glass cabinet, and silverware or ceramic pottery brought from the old country will always carry interesting stories.

Homes are the backdrops of our lives. Children register their first memories and experiences there. When they go out into the world, perhaps to form their own families, they can always turn back to that collection of memorable images and use them to build their own homes.

# HOUSING THE REST OF MY LIFE

ON MY FIFTIETH BIRTHDAY I DREW AN IMAGINARY LINE MARKING the beginning of the rest of my life. Triggered by the studies and housing designs for seniors that I'd done at the time, I placed myself in the text and the drawings I had created. I watched a person pushing a walker and wondered how I would walk years from now. I paused near the seniors' products aisle in the pharmacy, trying to figure out what each item was. I began thinking about my retirement savings and about writing a will. In a morning visit to the bathroom I stretched the skin down on my face, imagining what the years would do.

But as much as I tried I couldn't imagine myself an old man, slowing down and needing assisting devices. No wonder. In a society that glorifies youthful energy and beauty, who wants to think old? Still, I know that there will come a time when I won't be able to run as fast, carry as much, think as clearly, see as far, or hear as well. I'll have to succumb to the fact that I am old. Among the many things that I reflect on is where I'm going to live. Will my current dwelling conditions be sufficiently comfortable? And how long will I able to live independently at home? In other words, how will I house the rest of my life?

Not so long ago, "the rest of one's life" was relatively short. At the beginning of the twentieth century, old age was thought to set in at sixty-five, the mandatory retirement age for working people. That age was chosen as being sufficiently close to our life expectancy. When the Social Security Act was instituted in the United States in 1935, it decreed that a government pension would help out those people who lived beyond sixty-five and who couldn't support themselves through work. Not many reached that age, and most of those who did died shortly thereafter.

In old photos, people often looked much older than they really were. Dental hygiene wasn't common and prosthetic crowns were available only to the wealthy. Mass-marketed skin care products made their appearance only later in the century. Protection from the sun was unheard of, and regular exercising was advocated only years later. Reaching or passing the age of eighty made its way into families' unrecorded history. Cousins and aunts would talk with affection about Uncle Jack, who used to chop his own firewood and walk to the market every day, and who remembered the names of all family members on his deathbed at the age of eighty-five.

Recent medical advances have changed all that. The development of revolutionary procedures, treatments, and medicines represents an orchestrated effort not only to keep society healthy, but to stretch out life as long as medical wizardry permits. Bypass surgery has fixed defective hearts, cornea implants have given vision to the blind, and hip replacements have let the elderly walk again. And what with today's genetic exploration and organ harvesting, we can only speculate what life expectancy will be decades from now.

North Americans, in short, can expect to live longer than earlier generations. A lot longer, in fact. Forty years ago men were expected to live to age sixty-eight and women to seventy-four. By the year 2020, both men and women will live well into their eighties. (Yes, equality will prevail there too.) Statistics even show that those who reach their eighties will likely live well into their nineties. And it's projected that those sixty-five years and older will constitute 20 to 25 percent of the entire North American population. What, then, will be the makeup of this group?

One of the axioms of gerontology is that the elderly are heterogeneous, differing from one another with respect to their lifestyles, preferences, and physical and intellectual abilities. The years between fifty-five and eighty-five can't be lumped together and are commonly divided into age subgroups. But even there, not all those aged seventy-five, for example, are at the same mental and medical state. The two most recognized groups are the "young old," aged fifty-five to seventy-four, and the "old old," aged seventy-five and older.

All age groups experience a physical decline, of course, which over time will influence their ability to use and interact with objects and spaces at home. Age-related changes occur in almost every aspect of an older person's life and can be grouped into three major areas: psychological, social, and physical. Psychological changes may influence the ability to operate independently at home, to make choices, and to respond to emerging circumstances and opportunities. Privacy is also compromised as one gets older. The tendency is to place less importance on personal matters that earlier in life were closely guarded.

Socially, people don't change much as they get older. A friendly person will perhaps become more experienced and opinionated, but still remain friendly. Physical constraints, on the other hand, prevent old people from doing what they were comfortable with at an earlier stage. Continuing to foster a sense of belonging by being among family and friends, hopping into the car and visiting people across town, or flying to see a grandchild across the continent is, for many of the old-old group, a physical challenge.

Physiological changes have a direct impact on people's ability to use their homes and the features in them. As people age they gradually experience difficulty walking, maintaining postures for extended periods, reaching, and pushing and pulling doors or carts. Lifting or carrying 25 pounds (11 kilograms) is found to be a problem for women over the age of sixty-five.

Numerous changes in sensory processes occur as part of normal aging, and some of these changes have important implications for the use of spaces in homes. Color blindness and astigmatism, for example, erode the ability to see changes of level. Increased susceptibility to glare requires flooring and wall coverings that cut down the glare on reflective surfaces. It also has implications for lighting, as well as window treatments, appliances, picture frames and glass, and furniture. Deterioration of hearing is common; those over sixty-five are thirteen times more likely to use hearing aids than are younger people. Not being able to hear a doorbell, or a falling object or other warning sign, represents another source of danger in the house.

For those who wish to age independently at home, these physiological changes and their attendant risks will require reconsideration of home design in the coming years. As baby boomers begin to reach retirement age, housing is expected to become one of the most important issues for seniors and the home-building industry alike—some even point to the boom industries that will result. On the whole, the news is good: medical innovations will let people live long in relative comfort. Those who have inherited from earlier generations or invested well will be well off. However, economists suggest that most old people spend the remainder of their life savings in the last two years of their lives.

Some older people will continue to live in their huge houses after the kids have left. Last-time buyers will move into smaller units, a condo perhaps. Those who live in the northern part of the continent might get another place in the warm south. Others might move into new-style retirement communities where they'll be taken care of both medically and socially. Unsurprisingly, surveys show that most North Americans prefer to age at home rather than end their lives in an institution, to remain independent and in control for as long as they can. Their living places, therefore, will have to be adapted to the aging process.

Big and small changes are expected in North American homes. Guest rooms with an adjacent bathroom will reappear, built to host visiting kids and their families. Young retirees who embark on a new sign-off career will convert empty rooms into offices. New appliances and cabinets will be installed in many kitchens as boomers indulge in gourmet cooking. Sunrooms with skylights will help perk up low feelings and loneliness. Bathrooms will look more like spas as they assume a therapeutic role, easing aching bones with whirlpool baths and multi-jet or cascading shower stalls with adjustable seats. Side doors and grab bars to prevent slipping will also become common. Finally, exercise rooms with new brands of machines will help seniors stay fit and keep muscles stretched.

A new range of products will also influence interior design, including non-slip flooring, easy-grip handles for arthritis sufferers, and appliances with automatic shut-offs for those forgetful ones.

Other housing alternatives for seniors will be explored. The bi-generational home, for example, has been investigated in recent decades. It's not a new idea, of course; extended families certainly lived together prior to the Industrial Revolution, and immigrants to this continent commonly lived with their parents. Many still do. In some cultures, primarily Asian, the son is expected to care for his aging parents in his home; his wife accepts them as part of the marriage package, and they often look after the grandchildren while the parents are out working. In Japan, for example, where living with in-laws is common, prefab construction companies provide imaginative housing solutions for extended families. The buyers are offered a variety of designs and products that are meant to turn a portion of their space into a separate dwelling. The home is designed to become a single unit at a later stage.

Other types of multi-generational housing include the so-called "granny" flat, common in Australia. An independent structure, made either conventionally or prefabricated, is built at the back of an existing home. Ranging between 300 and 600 square feet (55 and 110 square meters), the unit contains a single bedroom, kitchenette, bathroom, and combination living and dining area. The elderly can enter the unit directly from the street or from the main house. Most North American municipalities have barred granny flats, fearing that these units, initially proposed as a temporary solution, will become permanent once the occupants have died. It's argued that they could become illegal rental units or some form of guest house.

The plex is a well-tried solution in Canada. Elders can live on the ground floor with the younger folks up above. Some models feature two entry doors, one for each unit. An interior passage and a staircase can even connect the units without residents having to go outside. Then there's the remodeling approach. A portion of an existing dwelling—a space in a two-car garage or a basement with its own entry, for example—can be converted into an independent unit. Again, the idea is that the two spaces could reunite in the distant future. Yet another approach is to create an independent, distinct space within the envelope of a new home. The two households share kitchen and dining spaces, but each has its own bedroom and bathroom arrangements.

Choosing among these alternatives will largely depend on budget and zoning allowances in each municipality. The net effect will be to keep the elderly active for as long as possible while providing them with independent living in society.

Many people who are planning their sunset years are even thinking about living in the same building with close friends. After all, these are the ones with whom they share experiences, memories, values, and future plans. I was once approached by three couples who consulted with me on designing a building where they could all live together upon their retirement. These people liked one another's company but also wanted to keep their privacy. I was as intrigued by the architectural challenge as I was by the social relationship—the whole prospect brought back memories of the 1960s communes.

When I began my design, I knew that avoiding stairs would be a significant consideration. The units, therefore, would have to be built on ground level and in a row. Another consideration was the group's desire for spaces they could all share. When I listed activities they could engage in together I realized that some of these could be on the main level and some below. A joint laundry room and a fitness room, for example, could be located in the basement. When the occupants got older and needed assistance, a nurse could be called in to provide round-the-clock supervision. An independent suite for the nurse could be constructed in the underground level with direct access to each of the units. In the years prior to engaging the nurse, the suite could house a visiting guest.

Watching movies or listening to music together could be another use for the underground level. Whereas building a theater-like screening room with a surround-sound system would be prohibitively expensive for a single occupant on a retirement income, the cost could be shared by a few. Another room could become a joint home office, with a computer, photocopier, fax machine, and scanner for common use. And then there are activities that can be done in common aboveground. A sunroom, much like a joint family room where they could have breakfast, read papers, and chat, could be another shared cost. The space could have a small kitchen, or at least a place where snacks can be prepared and coffee warmed up.

I'm reluctant to make detailed plans for my own future dwelling. I hope to stay independent at home as long as I can and to be as active as I can. I do like the bi-generational idea, and would welcome my son's or daughter's decision to live in our upper duplex unit. My wife and I won't mind babysitting the grandchildren from time to time.

# ACKNOWLEDGMENTS

My column "Forward Thinking," published since the year 2000 in the CanWest chain of newspapers, is where the seed idea for this book was planted. Special thanks, therefore, go to Toronto's Post Homes editors Jean Christmas and Tracy Picha, for giving me an opportunity and a podium, and also to Sheila Brady at the *Ottawa Citizen*.

Background material and research for the essays was the result of collaboration with many colleagues. Kim Albright, Stephanie Coleridge, Karen Hui, David Krawitz, Carmen Lee, and Thiago Valente worked on the Senneville project. Michael Wildman provided historical facts on the telephone and the internet. Jenifer Steffel collaborated in research on the genesis of cities and suburbs. Chuck Charlebois, Latimer Hu, Manon Lanctôt, Carmen Lee, and Richard Lu participated in the Cornwall project.

Vince Cammalleri collaborated on studies in energy efficiency, and Amanda Cooke on the Sears catalogue. Thanks go to Danny Cleary, who invited me to consult on the prefabricated plant venture, and to Nicola Bullock and Michelle Takoff for collaboration on the use of recycled products in the Grow Home.

The help of Nyd Garavito-Bruhn and David Krawitz in background research, typing, and editing earlier versions of this book is much appreciated. I would like to thank the McGill School of Architecture for giving me the time to write. Sincere thanks also go to my agent Robert Mackwood and editors Maria Scala, Karen Alliston, Sandra Tooze, and Eliza Marciniak at Penguin.

Finally, thanks to my family: my wife, Dr. Sorel Friedman, who offered ideas, edited essays, and was my companion in the voyage that led to the experiences described in this book, and to our children, Paloma and Ben.

# BIBLIOGRAPHY

## A HOME FIT FOR A QUEEN

Canada Mortgage and Housing Company (CMHC). *50 Years of Innovation, 1943–1993—The Canadian Housing Industry.* Ottawa: CMHC, 1993.

Jackson, K.T. *Crabgrass Frontier.* New York: Oxford University Press, 1985.

Statistics Canada. www.statcan.ca/english/Pgdb/famil66.htm.

Wright, G. *Building the American Dream.* Cambridge, MA: MIT Press, 1981.

## DORMERS IN DALIAN

Chimm, J. *The Village of Senneville.* Quebec: College of Geographic Sciences, 1995.

Marvin Windows and Doors. www.marvin.com.

Tafuri, Manfredo, and Francesco Dal Co. *Modern Architecture.* New York: Electra/Rizzoli, 1986.

Traquair, R. *The Old Architecture of Quebec: A Study of the Buildings Erected in New France from the Earliest Explorers to the Middle of the Nineteenth Century.* Toronto: Macmillan, 1947.

## TO KEEP OR NOT TO KEEP THE LIVING AND DINING ROOMS?

Jackson, K.T. *Crabgrass Frontier.* New York: Oxford University Press, 1985.

Ward, P. *A History of Domestic Space: Privacy and the Canadian Home.* Vancouver: University of British Columbia Press, 1999.

## A CONVERSATION WITH YOUR FRIDGE

Adler, J. "Take Out Nation." *Newsweek,* February 9, 2004.

## TIMELESS DESIGN

"The Adjustable House." *House and Home,* 2 (6) (December 1952),
114–116.

"Convertible Plan." *Architectural Forum,* (April 1949), 126–130.

Friedman, A. "The Evolution of Design Characteristics during the Post-
Second-World-War Housing Boom: The U.S. Experience." *Journal of
Design History,* 8 (2) (1995).

Marsan, J. *Montreal in Evolution.* Montreal: McGill-Queen's University
Press, 1990.

## HOMES WITH A GLOBAL REACH

Bell Telephone Company. *Telephone Service Provider.* 1918.

CIA World Fact Book. www.cia.gov/cia/publications/factbook/
geos/ca.html#Comm.

Fischer, S.C. *America Calling.* Berkeley: University of California Press,
1992.

Gizmodo. www.gizmodo.com/archives/laptop-sales-continue-to-grow-
008642.php.

Graham, S., and S. Marvin. *Telecommunications and the City: Electronic
Spaces, Urban Places.* New York: Routledge, 1996.

Nokia, Inc. www.nokia.ie/nokia/0,8764,29637,00.html.

Pool, I.S. *The Social Impact of the Telephone.* Cambridge, MA: MIT
Press, 1997.

U.S. Bureau of Labor Statistics. www.bls.gov/news.release/homey.nr0.htm.

U.S. Census Bureau. www.census.gov/prod/2004pubs/03statab/
inforcomm.pdf.

## DESIGNING FOR CIVILITY

Chonière, R. *Dossier Socio-Démographique et Sanitaire*. Montreal: CLSC NDG/Montréal-Ouest, 1990.

Congress of the New Urbanism (CNU), Kathleen McCormick, Robert Davis, and Shelley R. Poticha. *Charter of the New Urbanism: Region / Neighborhood, District, and Corridor / Block, Street, and Building*. New York: McGraw-Hill, 1999.

Howard, E. *Garden Cities of Tomorrow* (original 1898 title: *Tomorrow: A Peaceful Path to Real Reform*). London: Swan Sonnenschein and Co., 1902.

Jackson, F. *Sir Raymond Unwin: Architect, Planner and Visionary*. London: Zwemmer, 1985.

Macfayden, D. *Sir Ebenezer Howard and the Town Planning Movement*. Manchester: Manchester University Press, 1933.

Mumford, L. *The City in History: Its Origins, Its Transformations, and Its Prospects*. New York: Harcourt, 1961.

Stein, C.S. *Toward New Towns for America*. New York: Reinhold, 1957.

## REINVENTING CITIES

Bowering, I. *Bowering Guide to Eastern Ontario*. 1992.

Coffey, W.J. *The Evolution of Canada's Metropolitan Economies*. Montreal: The Institute for Research on Public Policy, 1994.

Daniels, T. *When City and Country Collide*. Washington, DC: Island Press, 1990.

Garreau, J. *Edge City: Life on the New Frontier*. New York: Doubleday, 1991.

Goldberg, M., and J. Mercer. *The Myth of the North American City: Continentalism Challenged*. Vancouver: University of British Columbia Press, 1986.

Jackson, K.T. *Crabgrass Frontier*. New York: Oxford University Press, 1985.

Kyte, E. *From Royal Township to Industrial City, Cornwall, 1784–1984*. Belleville: Mika Publishing, 1983.

McCullough, A.B. *The Primary Textile Industry in Canada: History and Heritage*. Ottawa: Minister of Supply and Services Canada, 1992.

## HOUSING THE TREES

Schumacher, E.F. *Small Is Beautiful: A Study of Economics as if People Mattered*. Point Roberts, WA: Hartley & Marks, 1973.

World Commission on Environment and Development. *Our Common Future*. Oxford: Oxford University Press, 1987.


## THEY DON'T BUILD THEM LIKE THEY USED TO

Eicher, N. *The Merchant Builders*. Cambridge, MA: MIT Press, 1982.

Home Depot, Inc. www.homedepot.com/HDUS/EN_US/corporate/about/global_presence.shtml.

Industry Canada. strategis.ic.gc.ca/epic/internet/inimr-ri.nsf/en/gr-77419e.html.

Rogers, E. *Diffusion of Innovations*. New York: Free Press, 1983.

Scanada Consultants Limited and Clayton Research Associates Ltd. *Three Decades of Innovation in Housing Technology: 1966–1996*. Prepared for CMHC, Ottawa, March 1996.

Statistics Canada Daily. December 2002. www.statcan.ca.


## WEATHERING THE STORM

Abley, M. *The Ice Storm: An Historic Record in Photographs of January 1998*. Toronto: McClelland & Stewart, 1998.

Boyle, G. *Renewable Energy: Power for a Sustainable Future*. Oxford: Oxford University Press, 1996.

Canada Mortgage and Housing Corporation (CMHC). *Energy Conservation in New Small Residential Buildings*. Ottawa: CMHC, 1981.

Canada Mortgage and Housing Corporation (CMHC). *Tap the Sun: Passive Solar Techniques and Home Designs*. Ottawa: CMHC, 1997.

Friedman, A., and V. Caummalleri. "Reducing Energy Resources and Construction Waste through Efficient Residential Unit Design." *Building Research and Information*, 22(2) (1994), 103–108.

Robinson, T. *Sustainable Housing for a Cold Climate*. Ottawa: Canada Mortgage and Housing Corporation, 1991.

Scanada Consultants Ltd. *Cost Benefit Evaluation and Environmental Influence of High Thermal Performance Windows in Canada, Energy Mines, and Resources*. Ottawa, 1992.


**A HOME IN A BOX**

Baristow, D. *Opportunities for Manufactured Housing in Canada*. Ottawa: Canada Mortgage and Housing Corporation, 1985.

Eichler, N. *The Merchant Builders*. Cambridge, MA: MIT Press, 1982.

Gans, H.J. *The Levittowners: Ways of Life and Politics in a New Suburban Community*. New York: Pantheon, 1967.

Herbert, G. *The Dream of the Factory-Made House: Walter Gropius and Konrad Wachsmann*. Cambridge, MA: MIT Press, 1984.

"Levitt's 1950 House." *Architectural Forum*, 92 (4) (April 1950), 136–137.

Robinson, S. *Manufactured Housing: What It Is, Where It Is, How It Operates*. Barrington, IL: Ingleside Publishing, 1988.

Sears, Roebuck and Company. *Sears and Roebuck Catalog of Houses, 1926: An Unabridged Reprint*. Philadelphia: Athenaeum of Philadelphia and Dover Productions, 1991.

Stevenson, K.C., and H.W. Jandi. *Houses by Mail: A Guide to Houses by Sears, Roebuck and Company*. New York: Preservation Press, 1986.


**A MARGARINE CONTAINER DECK**

Bullock, N., and M. Takoff. *Greening the Grow Home: The Use of Recycled Products in Building Materials.* Undergraduate Project Report, Department of Civil Engineering and Applied Mechanics. Montreal: McGill University, 1993.

Dobbs, D., and W. Talarico. "Turning Trash into Cash." *The Journal of Light Construction*, New England Edition. Richmond, VT (March 1991), 32–35.

Environment Canada. *Recycling in Canada* (April 1992).

Logsdon, G. "Agony and Ecstasy of Tire Recycling," *Biocycle*, (31) 7 (July 1990), 44–45, 84–85.

Office of Solid Waste Management (OSWM). "The Technology of Plastics Recycling." *Solid Waste Management,* 7 (7) (July 1993).

Robinson, W.D. *The Solid Waste Handbook*. New York: John Wiley & Sons, 1986.

Steuteville, R. "Recycled House Is Builder's Model." *Biocycle*, 34 (6) (June 1993), 64–65, 76.


## ACCEPTING THE ORANGE TILE

Blau, R.J. *The Architects and Films: A Sociological Perspective in Architectural Practice*. Cambridge, MA: MIT Press, 1984.


## BEAULIEU'S RACE

Canada Mortgage and Housing Corporation (CMHC). *Housing Export Opportunities Series*. Mexico, Ottawa: CMHC, 1997.

Friedman, A., M. Horvat, and M. Rojano. *Adapting Quebec Construction Products to Latin American Markets*. Montreal: McGill University School of Architecture, Affordable Homes Program, 1997.

Instituto Nacional de Estadistica, Geografica, y Informatica. *INEGI: About Mexico*, 1997. www.inegi.gob.mxhomeing/acerca/acrecademexico.html.


## HOUSING THE REST OF MY LIFE

Canada Mortgage and Housing Corporation. *Housing Choices for Older Canadians*. Ottawa: CMHC, n.d.

Pastalan, L. A. *Sensory Changes and Environmental Behavior, Design for Aging: A Comprehensive Package*. Washington, DC: American Institute of Architects/Association of Collegiate Schools of Architecture, 1992.

Pnoos, J., and S. Golant. "Housing and Living Arrangements for the Elderly." *Handbook of Aging and the Social Sciences*, 4th ed. Robert H. Binstock and Linda K. George, eds., 303–324. San Diego: Academic Press, 1995.

Regnier, V., and J. Pynoos (eds.). *Housing the Aged: Design Directives and Policy Considerations*. New York: Elsevier Science Publishing, 1987.

Schiff, M. *Special Design Considerations: Developing and Marketing Retirement Housing*. Toronto: Myra Schiff Consultants Corporation, n.d.

Steinfeld, E. *Adapting Housing for Older Disabled People, Design for Aging: A Comprehensive Package*. Washington, DC: American Institute of Architects/Association of Collegiate Schools of Architecture, 1992.

# ILLUSTRATION CREDITS

**A HOME FIT FOR A QUEEN, P. 2**
A contemporary single family home in suburban Montreal, Quebec.
© Avi Friedman, 2005

**DORMERS IN DALIAN, P. 12**
A 1912 home in Senneville, Quebec.
© Avi Friedman, 2005

**TO KEEP OR NOT TO KEEP THE LIVING AND DINING ROOMS? P. 22**
Christmas gathering, 254 Olivier Ave., Westmount, QC, 1899.
© Gift from Vennor Roper, MP-1977.76.99, Notman Photographic Archives, McCord Museum of Canadian History, Montreal, Quebec.

**A CONVERSATION WITH YOUR FRIDGE, P. 32**
Kitchen, C.B. Thorne's house, Montreal, QC, 1934.
© Purchased from Associated Screen News Ltd., VIEW-25411, Notman Photographic Archives, McCord Museum of Canadian History, Montreal, Quebec.

**OVERSIZED FURNITURE OR SMALL ROOMS? P. 42**
Living room sets on display in a Montreal furniture store.
© Avi Friedman, 2005

**TIMELESS DESIGN, P. 50**
Row of triplexes on Rue Drolet, Montreal, Quebec, constructed circa 1890.
© Avi Friedman, 2005

## HOMES WITH A GLOBAL REACH, P. 60

Apartment kitchen, Montreal, Quebec, circa 1947.

© Library and National Archives Canada, PA160615

## LIVING ABOVE THE STORE, P. 72

College Street facades, Toronto, Ontario.

© Judy Nisenholt, 2005

## DESIGNING FOR CIVILITY, P. 82

A park scene, Toronto, Ontario.

© Judy Nisenholt, 2005

## BRING BACK THE SCALE, P. 92

Street intersection in Meerlo, Holland.

© Avi Friedman, 2005

## REINVENTING CITIES, P. 104

Pitt Street looking north between 1st and 2nd Street, circa 1900.

Courtesy: Cornwall Community Museum/Archives, (613) 936-0842

## HOUSING THE TREES, P. 114

The first home in the forest of St. Nicolas.

© Avi Friedman, 2005

## THEY DON'T BUILD THEM LIKE THEY USED TO, P. 126

Johnston, Frances Benjamin (1864–1952). "Stairway of the Treasurer's Residence: Students work," plate from an album of Hampton Institute, Hampton, Virginia, U.S.A., 1899–1900. Platinum print, $7\frac{1}{2}$ x $9\frac{1}{2}$". Gift of Lincoln Kirstein. (859.1965.136). The Museum of Modern Art, New York, NY, U.S.A.

Digital Image © The Museum of Modern Art/Licensed by SCALA / Art Resource, NY

Illustration Credits

### WEATHERING THE STORM, P. 138

Firefighters in a Montreal neighbourhood during the Ice Storm, 1998.

© Richard Arless Jr./*The Gazette* (Montreal)

### A HOME IN A BOX, P. 148

The PALMYRA, one of *Sears Catalog* Homes, 1918.

Courtesy: Sears, Roebuck and Co. (The image is reprinted by arrangement with Sears, Roebuck and Co.).

### A MARGARINE CONTAINER DECK, P. 158

Clay brick ready for recycling at a Habitat for Humanity ReStore in Saskatoon, Saskatchewan, Canada.

© Avi Friedman, 2005

### ACCEPTING THE ORANGE TILE, P. 170

No title; the rendering appeared in an advertising brochure for a Montreal flooring company circa 1940.

Author unknown.

### BEAULIEU'S RACE, P. 182

A home in a squatter settlement near Tijuana, Mexico.

© Avi Friedman, 2005

### OUR FIRST HOME, P. 194

Residents in front of their new Grow Homes in Aylmer, Quebec, 1988.

© Avi Friedman, 2005

### DESIGN FOR FAMILY LIFE, P. 206

Thanks before eating, 1864, painting copied for Watson Art Gallery.

© Purchased from Associated Screen News, Ltd., VIEW-26161, Notman Photographic Archives, McCord Museum of Canadian History, Montreal.

### HOUSING THE REST OF MY LIFE, P. 214

Older gentlemen sitting around a park table, Toronto, Ontario.

© Judy Nisenholt, 2005